Don't Be A Victim!
How to Protect Yourself
from
Hoaxes, Scams, and Frauds

by Michael E. Chesbro

Loompanics Unlimited
Port Townsend, Washington

Neither the author nor the publisher assumes any responsibility for the use or misuse of information contained in this book. It is sold for informational purposes only. Be Warned!

Don't Be A Victim!

How to Protect Yourself from Hoaxes, Scams, and Frauds
© 2002 by Michael E. Chesbro

Published by:
Loompanics Unlimited
PO Box 1197
Port Townsend, WA 98368
Loompanics Unlimited is a division of Loompanics Enterprises, Inc.
Phone: 360-385-2230
E-mail: service@loompanics.com
Web site: www.loompanics.com

ISBN 1-55950-230-4
Library of Congress Card Catalog Number 2002109259

Contents

Dedication

For Joni, Skye, Tommi and Max

Introduction

Hoaxes, scams, frauds... tens of thousands of people become victims of these crimes every year. But how can so many people be conned out of their life savings, be tricked into paying for products and services they will never receive, or even lose their complete identity to these criminals?

There is an old saying: "You can't cheat an honest man." While it is certainly much easier to take advantage of someone who tries to get something for nothing, honest people of good character regularly become the victims of hoaxes, scams, and frauds.

There are perhaps many reasons why one can fall victim to these crimes, but probably the leading reason these crimes are so successful is a lack of personal privacy. The average person today is willing to disclose to an absolute stranger what should be private and personal information. We tolerate government and corporate intrusion into our private lives, suffering greater and greater loss of our rightful liberties in the name of bureaucracy or some politician's pork-barrel project.

We have become so used to disclosing private information about our lives at every turn that when someone asks us for our Social Security number, bank account number, or the like, we don't see these inquiries as the risk and intrusion into our lives that they are. Too often we answer these questions without the slightest thought about the damage that can be done with this information. We lock our front doors to keep a burglar from breaking in, but do nothing to prevent a criminal from stealing our personal and private information and maybe our complete identities.

In this book we will look at various different hoaxes, scams, and types of fraud. We will learn to recognize these crimes for what they are and we will look at things we can do to protect ourselves from becoming victims of these crimes.

It is important to remember, however, that no book can identify every possible hoax, scam, or fraud or every variation on these crimes. There will always be some new twist, some new way that criminals find to take advantage of the unsuspecting.

What we can do, is learn to recognize a few of the most common of these crimes, and to recognize the underlying principles that make these crimes successful. With this awareness, and by taking certain common sense precautions, we can shield ourselves from these crimes, causing the criminals to move on to the many people who don't take this threat seriously!

Chapter One
Internet Scams

Have you heard that the government plans to institute a tax on e-mail? The details of this upcoming law can be found in Federal Bill 602P, sponsored by Congressman Tony Schnell (R). This new law will have a major impact on the way we do business and should be addressed by any organization or individual who relies on e-mail for business or personal correspondence.

The FBI National Gang Task Force has issued a warning about a spreading gang-initiation ritual. Gang members drive around at night with their vehicle lights off (or on high-beam) until an approaching motorist flashes his own lights at the gang members to indicate that they should turn on or dim their lights. This individual now becomes the target of the gang member to be initiated, who must catch up with the passing motorist and shoot him (or at least fire shots into his vehicle).

The Centers for Disease Control and Prevention issued a warning about AIDS-infected needles being placed in coin-return slots of vending machines, in the seats at movie theaters, and other locations where people get stuck by them and become infected with AIDS.

The Federal Communications Commission (FCC) issued a warning this week about a new computer virus called "Good Times." The Good Times virus is transmitted through e-mail and will put your computer's processor into an nth-complexity infinite binary loop, causing severe damage to the computer hardware and resulting in the loss of any data stored on the system.

Hoaxes and Warnings

Do any of the above warnings sound familiar to you? Perhaps you have received a copy of one or more of these warnings in your e-mail. Maybe you passed it on to friends, family, and associates to warn them of potential danger. Unfortunately, if you passed along any of these warnings (or many others like them), you are the victim of an Internet hoax and you helped perpetrate that hoax by passing along the bogus warning.

Many people who look at these hoaxes/warnings believe them because they appear to come from legitimate sources, contain what appears to be specific facts, and often contain technical-sounding language, leading the victim of the hoax to believe that the author of the warning must know what he is talking about. These bogus warnings take on a greater air of legitimacy when a respected institution or person (such as a company security manager), who is looked to for accurate information, passes them on.

Signs of a Hoax

Generally, Internet hoaxes have certain features that distinguish them from legitimate information.

- There is usually a plea that we pass the warning on to as many people as possible.
- There is almost never a verifiable point-of-contact or originating source of the message. In the rare case where there is a point-of-contact or originating source listed, it is usually fake.
- There are often easily verifiable factual errors in hoax messages (Congressman Tony Schnell or the FCC disseminating computer virus information).

If you think that there is a possibility that the warning is real, at least take time to verify the information before you pass it on. If it's not worth the effort to research the warning, it's probably not worth forwarding it to everyone in your address book. Often when we take a minute to look carefully at the information contained in these hoaxes, it quickly becomes clear what they are.

Look at the warning about an upcoming e-mail tax. Common sense should tell us that there is no technical infrastructure in place that would allow the government to implement such a tax, even if it wanted to do so. However, assuming that you believe the technology is available, just what is Federal Bill 602P? Any schoolboy knows that bills before Congress and the Senate are not titled "Federal Bill." If you slept through all your American government classes in grade school, you can still confirm that the sponsor of the bill, Tony Schnell, is not actually a member of Congress. All congressional representatives are listed on the Office of the Clerk Web site (among many other places), available online at: clerkweb.house.gov/main.htm. There is no Congressman Tony Schnell (nor has there ever been), which is a pretty good clue that he couldn't have sponsored this nonexistent bill.

Okay, so there was no e-mail tax bill, but what about the Good Times virus? We all know that there are computer viruses, but the Federal Communications Commission doesn't send out e-mail warnings about them. That's simply not the job of the FCC. Furthermore, just what is an "nth-complexity infinite binary loop"? Don't know? Neither does anyone else. It sounds like some major technical problem, but in actuality there is no such thing. It's just something invented for the hoax, or perhaps something that Klingon computers do on *Star Trek*. Yet millions of people were duped into believing in the Good Times virus and passed along the hoax warning to everyone in their e-mail address books.

Isn't it better to be safe than sorry? If I receive a warning that seems to make sense, isn't it better to pass it along than to ignore something that might be a real threat? Absolutely not. Besides contributing to the mass of Internet junk mail out there, passing along bogus warnings tends to cause people to ignore real warnings. Remember the fable about the boy who cried wolf?

Consider how quickly a hoax message can multiply. If everyone who receives the hoax message passes it on to just ten others, by the time it has reached just the sixth generation, one million copies of this bogus message have passed across the Internet.

Most of us have far more than ten addresses in our e-mail address book, and when sending out a general warning, tend to send it to everyone. It is likely that there will be far more than one million copies of a message passed by the sixth generation, even if everyone who receives it isn't duped into passing it on to others.

Once we have more than one million copies of a hoax warning in circulation, it starts to take a toll on business and operational efficiency. Erroneous decisions are made because of the hoax, and corporate security departments, information technology managers, and health officials have to address concerns based on the hoax. This results in a waste of time and money that could be better spent dealing with real threats, actual information technology problems, and true health concerns.

With regard to the Good Times hoax, so many people contacted the FCC about their nonexistent warning and this nonexistent virus, that the FCC finally had to research the matter and issue the following official statement:

May 3, 1995

Alleged "Good Times" Virus

A rumor has been circulating on the Internet and other on-line services, that the "FCC" released a public notice warning about an alleged "Good Times" computer virus. The U.S. Federal Communications Commission (U.S. FCC) did not issue such a notice. This rumor has recycled several times in the last few months.

The U.S. FCC does not disseminate information regarding the existence, impact, or effect of computer viruses. Information regarding the alleged "Good Times" virus is available in:

DOE, CIAC Notes 95-09 dated April 24, 1995 by contacting the Department of Energy (DOE), Computer Incident Advisory Capability (CIAC) at E-mail: ciac@llnl.gov or call (501) 422-8193, or

Department of Defense (DoD) users can contact Automated Systems Security Incident Support Team (ASSIST) at E- mail: assist@assist.mil or call (800) 357-4231 or local (703) 607-4700, or DSN 327-4700, reference 95-15, E-Mail Virus is a Hoax, dated April 24, 1995. One of the missions of ASSIST is to offer DoD user support in matters relating to security and vulnerability issues.

For questions or comments, call Sheryl Segal (202) 418-0265.

-FCC-

There are several resources available on the Internet for checking on potential hoaxes. If you receive some type of warning message, before you decide to pass it along and possibly contribute to the spread of false information, check its veracity with these resources.

* Computer Incident Advisory Center:
  hoaxbusters.ciac.org/

- McAfee: vil.mcafee.com/hoax.asp

- Symantec (Norton):
  www.symantec.com/avcenter/hoax.html

- Vmyths: www.vmyths.com/

- Data Fellows (F-Secure):
  www.europe.f-secure.com/virus-info/hoax/

- Centers For Disease Control's Health Hoaxes:
  www.cdc.gov/hoax_rumors.htm

- NonProfit Net:
  www.nonprofit.net/hoax/default.htm

Reasons for Hoaxes

Why would anyone want to start an Internet hoax? The originator of the hoax is almost never identified to the victims of the hoax. Perhaps the most common reason is to see just what one can get away with. How far can one get the hoax to spread? Even though the originator of the hoax is almost never identified in the hoax itself, the individual originating the hoax, and perhaps a few of his close friends, know about it and likely get a laugh out of the number of people who fall for their lies.

Another fairly common reason to start a hoax is to use it as a means of harassment against a specific individual or business. A hoax with a spoofed e-mail header or a false point-of-contact listed in the text of the message can result in hundreds or even thousands of e-mail replies or calls being directed to an individual or business that has no responsibility for or knowledge of the hoax itself. A hoax may also be intended to damage the reputation of a business or organization by spreading false and misleading information.

Finally, online hoaxes may be part of a larger scam to bilk money out of unsuspecting victims. These hoaxes are the most dangerous to the individual, because they are specifically trying to gain access to your accounts or have you provide funds for something you are unlikely to ever receive.

There will always be those individuals who feel the need to pass along information to everyone in their e-mail address book. This is much like the neighborhood gossip who passes along little pieces of information without really knowing the facts or bothering to confirm the information. If you really must pass along the latest Internet warning, plea, or gossip, at least take a couple of minutes to be sure that you are not contributing to an online hoax. Before passing along any e-mail message, add the following information to the top of the message you are sending.

- *I received this message from* _____ . Include the name and e-mail address of the individual from whom you received the message. Things like "a good friend," "Doc," or "one of my guys" have no place here. The intent is to allow those who receive the message from you to contact the originator of the message.

- *I have confirmed the validity of the information in this message by* _____ . List any Web sites, telephone contact numbers, or other sources you used to confirm the information you are passing along. Anyone receiving the message from you should be able to view the same confirming sources that you list.

* *I am passing along this message because* _____.
Clearly state why you feel it is important to disseminate the information you are sending.

If you cannot identify who sent the message to you or originated the message, have not been able to confirm the information with other sources, and cannot state clearly why you are passing the information on to others, you should not forward the information. Doing so is probably just contributing to some online hoax or scam. If, on the other hand, you can complete the three brief statements above and add them to the message, you are likely distributing information that is at least somewhat useful.

If everyone simply took the time to add the above three statements to any e-mail they forwarded, it would greatly reduce the number of online hoaxes. If it's not worth the time to confirm the information in the message and add the header information, the message is not worth passing on to others.

Spam Equals Scam

If you have an e-mail account, sooner or later you will receive spam (unsolicited commercial e-mail). Spam is the electronic equivalent of junk mail. It hawks everything from "get rich quick" schemes, real estate offers, and medication, to pornography, or just about anything else you can think of.

Unfortunately, spam is almost always a scam. If you actually respond to unsolicited commercial e-mail and send money for whatever product or service it is hawking, there is a forty-five to sixty-five percent chance that you will receive nothing at all for your money. If, by some chance, you do receive a product ordered from an unsolicited commercial e-mail, there is about a ninety-five percent chance that it will be a product of inferior quality and not worth the money you paid for it.

Does this mean that one should never shop online and that every sales offer sent by e-mail is completely bogus? Of course not. Many very reputable businesses have Web sites and offer their customers the chance to receive advertising and special offers by e-mail. However, every reputable business sending advertising via e-mail does so only to those customers who have requested it. These reputable businesses, when sending e-mail advertisements, clearly indicate in the subject line of the e-mail their company name and the fact that the e-mail is an advertisement of some kind. Also, the body of the e-mail will contain the company's name, address, and telephone number. There may also be links to various products on the company's Web site, but no legitimate, reputable business sending e-mail advertising requires you to click on any link or visit any Web site to identify contact information. Furthermore, if you reply to the e-mail advertisement by return e-mail, a legitimate business will receive that reply — that is, the return path will be valid. In the case of spam and its associated scams and fraud, replying to the e-mail address from which the spam was sent will usually result in undeliverable e-mail. In other cases, the return path is forged so that the person receiving your reply is not the originator of the spam.

Identifying Spam

There are some very good clues to help you identify e-mail solicitation that is nothing more than a scam.

1. You did not request that you receive advertising or information from the company sending you the e-mail.
2. You have no pre-existing relationship with the company.
3. The subject line is misleading.
4. The text does not clearly identify the company sending the e-mail and does not provide accurate contact information for the company. It might ask you to click on links to locate this information.
5. Your e-mail address is not contained in the To: line of the header.
6. The return path and the From: address in the e-mail header do not match or at least have the same domain name.
7. The return path — or "reply to" addresses— and links to request removal from future e-mail are associated with free e-mail services (such as Hotmail, Yahoo, etc.).

The most important giveaway that e-mail advertising is some kind of a scam is the first item on the list above: You did not request that you receive advertising or information from the company sending you the e-mail. If you did not request the information be sent to you via e-mail, and it tries to get you to buy a product or service, or visit a Web site to do the same, it is spam, and in almost all cases "spam equals scam!"

Remember that any company that uses misleading and unsolicited e-mail to sell their products or services is acting in an irresponsible manner. Do you really expect to receive a quality product or reliable service from this type of company? You might also want to consider how the company sending spam to your e-mail account got your address in the first place. What kind of online snooping are they using to cull e-mail addresses for their spam e-mail anyway? Obviously, if they are acquiring your e-mail address from someone other than you, it is probably a very bad idea to conduct business with this company. You almost certainly didn't provide your e-mail address to someone with the intent of having a company steal it for the purpose of sending spam e-mail.

Reporting Spam

You should resolve never to purchase any product or service as a result of spam — it's probably a scam anyway. Don't click on any links in spam e-mail or visit any Web sites listed in the spam. Finally, make it a point to report spam to your Internet Service Provider (ISP) and other organizations and agencies working to stop this online criminal activity. Three useful places, in addition to your ISP, to report spam are:

1. The attorney general of your state. The attorneys general of many states will take action against a

"spammer" if they receive a sufficient number of complaints from the residents of their state.
2. The FBI's Internet Fraud Complaint Center at: www1.ifccfbi.gov/index.asp
3. The Better Business Bureau

In May 2001, the FBI's Internet Fraud Complaint Center and the National White Collar Crime Center announced the results of its battle against online fraud, a program called "Operation Cyber Loss." This operation exposed online criminal activity affecting 56,000 victims who suffered a cumulative loss of more than $117 million. Operation Cyber Loss resulted in fifty-seven arrests and more than 110 counts of wire fraud, mail fraud, bank fraud, telemarketing fraud, conspiracy to commit fraud, money laundering, software piracy, and transfer of stolen property.

Operation Cyber Loss was certainly a success, and the FBI and National White Collar Crime Center should be applauded for their efforts, but this is only the tip of a very large iceberg. Looking at the statistics from Operation Cyber Loss we see that fifty-seven people were able to victimize more than 56,000. To protect ourselves from becoming victims of these crimes, it is essential that we report spam and related indicators of this massive, ongoing criminal activity.

Reporting spam helps your ISP develop protocols to screen out spam, protect your e-mail account, and limit online fraud. Reporting it to consumer protection services aids in putting these criminals out of business. Spammers must come to realize that sending unsolicited commercial e-mail will only result in a boycott of the product or service they are hawking and complaints being filed about them with

ISPs and consumer protection services. Take the Anti-Spam Pledge:

> *I will never purchase any product or service from a company that sends spam (unsolicited commercial e-mail). I will report spam to my Internet Service Provider (ISP) and other organizations fighting this online criminal activity.*

Some criminals sending spam will try to make it look like a response to information you have requested. The e-mail will say things such as "Here Is The Information You Requested" in the subject line, or "Here Are The Results of Your Feedback Form." You know that you didn't request this information, but the goal of the spammer is to get you to open and read the e-mail. Since the subject line of the spam is a lie — you didn't request the information — do you expect the contents of the message to be anything more than a lie?

A Spam Experiment

While researching this book, I conducted some brief experiments with spam in an attempt to identify whether it was being used by any legitimate business. First, I established a new account with a major ISP. I then used this account to "surf the Internet," enter a couple of online chats, and establish an e-mail address, making a few purchases from the Web sites of well-established companies. I simply used the new account as any average user might, but without employing any anti-spam software or screening.

Within a week after I established the account, the spam began to arrive. At first it was just a couple of messages. I made it a point to use the "remove me" link on any spam e-mail which contained one. On all spam e-mail that I opened, I used the "reply" button in my browser to send an e-mail back to the sender asking to be removed from their e-mail list. This usually resulted in undeliverable e-mail. Spam, whose subject line indicated that it was pornographic, I deleted without opening. All others, including pornographic spam that I opened because the subject line was false or misleading, received a request to be removed from their e-mail list.

A few offers that were potentially legitimate (investments, products, travel, etc.) received a response requesting more information. I even invested $100 in this experiment, sending off money orders to a few of these spam advertisers for their products or information packets.

What did I learn from this brief experiment? First, never attempt to purchase anything advertised in spam. In six instances where I sent between $6.90 and $29.95 for spam-advertised products, I received absolutely nothing. In one of the six cases, I received an e-mail stating my item was on backorder. I have heard nothing since from that company, and the e-mail address from which I received the backorder message is no longer valid.

Using the "remove me" links included in some spam e-mail did not remove me from these lists. In fact, it actually seemed to increase the amount of spam I received. Simply put, it showed these spammers that my e-mail address was valid and that I opened the spam and read it, at least with enough thoroughness to find the "remove me" link.

Using the "reply" button in my browser to respond to the spam mail and ask that I be removed from their e-mail list was totally ineffective. In most cases, the reply simply did not work. The address in the reply block was invalid. This should be a strong clue to anyone considering an advertisement sent by unsolicited commercial e-mail. If the e-mail address sending the spam is invalid, the product or service being advertised is also going to be invalid.

By the end of the experiment — about two months later — my account was receiving an average of forty spam messages every day. This made it very difficult to use the account to send and receive normal e-mail. Any e-mail I wanted to receive was buried in the mass of spam and often missed. At the end of the third month, I had to close the account, because it was totally unusable due to the constant flood of spam.

Spam is a scam. It is massive, online criminal activity. If you attempt to actually purchase a product you learn about through unsolicited commercial e-mail, you will almost certainly lose your money. If you attempt to reply to the senders of spam and ask that you be removed from their list, it will only increase the amount of spam you receive.

Spam will continue to be a problem until we take direct action against the companies that conduct this criminal activity. Take the "Anti-spam Pledge" and report all spam to consumer protection agencies. Demand that your elected representatives take legal action against these criminals. And remember that spam is a scam.

Area Code 809 Fraud

One type of fraud that may be associated with Internet hoaxes is international telephone calling fraud. The way this works is that you will receive an e-mail, or other type of communication (such as a number on your pager), requesting that you call a number in the 809 (or other non-U.S.) area code. The e-mail message could be something like this:

Top Watch Company

Congratulations — Your name has been chosen as one of our grand prize winners! Call 1-809-123-4567 to claim your prize. No Credit Card Necessary. No Shipping or Postal Fees. Claim your prize with one simple telephone call. 1-809-123-4567.

You may not remember entering any contest, but it's only a phone call and you obviously seem to have won some type of prize. What can it hurt? So you make the call and listen to a recorded message, or maybe you are transferred to a person who keeps you on the line or puts you on hold. The whole point with this scam is to keep you on the line as long as possible. While you are on the line you are being billed for an international call.

Area code 809 isn't in the United States; it's in the Dominican Republic. Starting in 1958, several countries and territories in the Caribbean were assigned area code 809, following the North American dialing plan, so 809 included all the Caribbean islands. By the mid-1990s, area code 809 was becoming overloaded, so additional area codes were assigned, giving each country and territory its own area code.

As a result, there are now several numbers, which one might assume to be in the United States, but which are actually international calls.

Area Code	Country/Territory
264	Anguilla
268	Antigua & Barbuda
242	Bahamas
246	Barbados
441	Bermuda (Atlantic)
284	British Virgin Islands
345	Cayman Islands
767	Dominica
809	Dominican Republic
473	Grenada & Carriacou
876	Jamaica
664	Montserrat
787 & 939	Puerto Rico
869	St. Kitts & Nevis
758	St. Lucia
784	St. Vincent & the Grenadines
868	Trinidad & Tobago
649	Turks & Caicos Islands
340	U.S. Virgin Islands

With the new assigned area codes, the 809 area code scam may take on a new twist and need a new name, but the scam is much the same.

Collecting the Cash

How does someone make money from this scam? One way comes from the fact that some numbers in these Caribbean area codes are "pay-per-call" numbers, much like 900-numbers in the United States. U.S. law requires that calls to pay-per-call numbers tell you what you are being charged for the call and allow you to hang up without being charged during the first minute of the call. In the non-U.S. countries of the Caribbean, there may be no such requirement.

A second possibility comes from the way international calls are handled. The Caribbean criminals may have an arrangement with their telephone service to receive a portion of fees charged for calls routed to their number(s). This "kickback" from the telephone company may be perfectly legal (or perhaps overlooked) outside of the United States. Either way, you end up being billed for the call.

Remember, once you have made the call, it is the criminal's plan to keep you on the line as long as possible. While you are listening to a recording, waiting on hold, or even talking to someone, thinking you are paying seven to ten cents per minute for your call, you are being billed for an international call at maybe a couple dollars per minute, or a pay-per-call charge of seven to ten dollars (or more) per minute.

Try explaining to your telephone company that you are not responsible for the international call fees or the $70-$100 in pay-per-call charges on your next telephone bill. Even if they were sympathetic to your plight and wanted to conduct some type of investigation, these numbers are not in the United States. The individual(s) running this scam from, say, the Dominican Republic, may technically not even be violating the law there.

Finally, while $70-$100 is a lot of money to have tacked onto your telephone bill, it is not so significant that you are likely to spend a great deal of effort fighting it. After complaining to your local telephone company, maybe even filing a report with the police and various fraud divisions, many people simply end up paying the bill. The criminals committing this type of telephone fraud know this, and this is why this type of fraud continues.

Does this mean that you should never call a number in the 809 area code or one of the other area codes listed above? You may have very legitimate reasons for calling one of these area codes, and you may be in a position to receive legitimate requests to make calls to these countries. Just be aware, before placing a call to a number that you don't recognize, that it may be an international call and it may be part of a scam.

Advance Fee Scam
(Nigerian Scam)

Another scam often associated with the Internet and with mass mailing is the Nigerian Letter Scam, also known as the Advanced Fee Scam. The name comes from the fact that for many years there has been a group working out of Nigeria and using this scam to con individuals out of their hard-earned cash.

The Nigerian Scam works like this: You receive an e-mail — or perhaps a letter posted from Nigeria — claiming to be from a representative in the Ministry of Oil and Gas, the Ministry of Mines, or some other position in the government. The letter explains that the sender has a considerable amount of money that he needs to move out of the country to protect it from the current corrupt government. This money is from various Nigerian government accounts totaling several million dollars.

So what do you have to do to get your share of these millions? You are supposed to let these Nigerian officials transfer millions of dollars through your bank account, for which you will receive a percentage. That's right, just give them access to your account so they can put money into it.

Does giving access to your bank accounts to someone you have never even met sound like an incredibly stupid idea? It should, but a great number of people did just that. They gave these Nigerian criminals access to their bank accounts in hopes of receiving a portion of these transferred funds.

Once they have you on the hook, they hint broadly that the money transfer is illegal. Of course, the Nigerian government is opposed to the transfer of this money, but it may also violate U.S. tax laws or money-laundering laws. The idea is to make you hesitate to report any initial suspicions you may have to the authorities.

If you actually give these criminals access to accounts containing any amount of money, you will find that they make withdrawals instead of the promised deposits. Perhaps you open a new account for this transfer. Soon after providing the account information to our Nigerian con men, you receive a communication that the money is being transferred. As you are about to go down to the bank and check on the millions of dollars in your account, you receive another communication letting you know there has been some kind of a holdup of the transfer. The funds have been blocked, there is a transfer fee, or there is some other reason. Of course the problem can be quickly resolved if you are willing to pay the transfer fee. How much? Well, it's $10,000. Can you come up with that much? No? How about half? The Nigerians will find a way to come up with the other $5,000. You'll have the transfer fee back one hundred times over as soon as the money is transferred. It should only take a day once the transfer fee is paid. They have to move quickly in order to transfer the money. Can you wire the money today?

As you read about this scam, you may be wondering how many people would fall for something like this. In fact, a great number of people fell for this scam. In 2001, the National Fraud Information Center reported that the Nigerian Scam ranked among the top three Internet crimes, with victims averaging a loss of $5,957 each!

The Bogus Prize

However, the advanced fee scam doesn't have to involve millions of dollars and Nigerians. Anything that requires that you pay money in advance in order to receive some kind of prize or benefit, can be part of an advanced fee scam.

It's Saturday morning. You're working on that second cup of coffee when the telephone rings.

"Hello, Mr. Wilson. Congratulations! You have been selected as one of the grand prize winners of the WeConU Sweepstakes. Yes, sir. You've won $25,000! Our prize awards committee is waiting to deliver your winnings. All you need to do is sign the release to allow us to use your name in future advertising and pay the federal taxes on the prize. The taxes are only ten percent, just $2,500. We can have our courier pick up the tax payment this afternoon, and as soon as it's processed, our prize awards committee will present your $25,000 check."

Does this sound a little more believable than a bunch of Nigerians wanting to launder millions of dollars through your bank account? People win sweepstakes every day. As for the taxes, of course, the IRS will demand the money up front. But you're no fool. You've signed the releases, but you kept copies of them for your records. You've got paperwork showing that you're the winner of the $25,000 prize. You've even got a telephone number to call back to the sweepstakes committee.

If you paid the taxes — you've been conned. There is no prize. Legitimate sweepstakes will never require that you pay money in order to claim a prize. Taxes may certainly be withheld from the total amount paid to you, but you will not be required to give up anything in order to claim a prize. If the contest is legitimate, there will be no advanced fee!

The advanced fee scam can be presented in any number of different ways, but the concept is always the same. A large amount of money or some object of value is guaranteed to you, but in order to claim it there is some "minimal" fee involved.

This scam is fairly easy to defend against. Never pay an advanced fee in order to receive a prize or a sum of money. The problem is that the criminals running this con convince the victim that his valuable prize or a large sum of money is just around the corner. Of course, there is no prize waiting for the victims of these criminals, but the scam works because there are always people who will believe the smooth-talking con man.

If you are ever told that you must pay an advanced fee in order to receive a prize, it's a scam.

Chapter Two
Check Scams

When you think of check scams, one of the first things that comes to mind is likely to be bounced checks, that is, criminals writing checks knowing they have insufficient funds in their account or that the account is closed, and then disappearing with the merchandise or cash obtained with the worthless check. This type of crime does happen and will be discussed later, but there is another scam involving checks that can leave you in financial ruin. This other check scam is the gathering of personal information on your check, for purposes of identity theft.

Disclosure of Your Personal Information

Think for a minute about the information currently on the face of your personal checks. There is the name and address of your bank and your checking account number. Your own name and address are most likely also preprinted on your checks, and maybe your telephone number, Social Security number, driver's license number, and more. Add to this the fact that when you write a check, you sign it, giving a clear example of your signature, and I have everything I need to steal your identity and your life savings, and run up bills in your name that you may never completely resolve!

To protect yourself against this type of crime, you may want to simply avoid using personal checks for direct retail purchases. Pay cash or use a check debit card. Most places that accept checks are also set up to accept credit and debit cards. If you do choose to write a personal check for a direct retail purchase, be absolutely certain that your Social Security and/or driver's license numbers are not preprinted on your checks, and don't let the merchant copy that information onto the check. Anyone who understands how recovery of insufficient funds checks works knows that your Social Security number or driver's license number on the check does nothing to aid in recovery of funds, but it can certainly aid in identity theft and fraud against you personally. We are warned over and over again not to allow our Social Security number or driver's license number to be recorded on our checks. Nevertheless, unwitting individuals still print these numbers on their checks and sleazy merchants still demand these numbers as a condition of writing a personal check, putting their customers at risk.

In his book *Scam School* (MacMillan, 1997), nationally recognized investigative reporter Chuck Whitlock warns: "Never allow a merchant to record your driver's license, Social Security, or credit card number on your check; if they insist upon it, pay by cash or credit card, or shop somewhere else" (p. 96). This same warning is echoed by the Federal Deposit Insurance Corporation (FDIC) in the *FDIC Consumer News*, Fall 1997 article, "Your Wallet: A Loser's

Manual." An *InfoPlease* article (www.infoplease.com) titled, "How To Stop Thieves From Using Your Checks," citing the FDIC as its source, again warns about the dangers of putting your Social Security or driver's license numbers on your checks. The article warns: "These numbers, combined with other information on your checks (your name, address, account number, telephone number) could supply a thief with enough details to apply for a loan, credit card, or a phony bank account in your name."

The National Association of Independent Insurers warns about printing your driver's license number on your checks, as do many banks (such as the Bank of Verona, Verona, WI, and the Michigan Credit Union League). In their anti-fraud tips, published on their Web site, Washington Mutual Bank says, "Don't include information such as your driver's license or Social Security numbers on your pre-printed checks."

Furthermore, state attorneys general advise residents of their states to restrict the amount of information recorded on their checks. As just one example, the Attorney General of Indiana warns: "When you order new checks, consider removing 'extra' information such as your Social Security number, assigned driver's license number, middle name, and telephone number. The less personal-identifying information you make available, the more likely an identity thief will choose an easier target."

Finally, the organizations dedicated to fighting check fraud give us the same warning. The National Check Fraud Center, in its *Check Fraud Prevention Tips,* states: "Limit the amount of personal information on your check. For example, do not include your Social Security, driver's license, or tele-

Don't Be A Victim!
How to Protect Yourself from Hoaxes, Scams, and Frauds

30

phone numbers on your check. A criminal can use this information to literally steal your identity by applying for a credit card or loan in your name, or even open a new checking account."

Simply put, having your driver's license or Social Security numbers pre-printed on your checks, or allowing a merchant to record these numbers on your check during the course of a transaction, is foolish and leaves the door wide open for fraud and identity theft directed against you. It should be clear from the repeated warnings cited above, along with many others not repeated here, that associating your Social Security number or driver's license number with your checks can only cause you harm.

Driver's License Numbers

What if you are a merchant and take checks as a courtesy to your customers who want to use them? You demand Social Security numbers and driver's license numbers on the checks so you can follow up if someone gives you a bad check. There's nothing underhanded going on here. You are just trying to protect your business.

That may be, but such demands for ID numbers seem closer to Nazi Germany's Gestapo demanding "Papers, Please" than to customer courtesy. Even so, I contacted my state Department of Motor Vehicles (DMV) and asked them whether they would release information from an individual's DMV record to help a merchant recover a bad check. The DMV responded that they could not release any information from an individual's DMV record in this case, stating: "The Federal Driver's Privacy Protection Act, 18 USC 2721 and our state law limits who we can release information to, and in most cases prohibits releasing personal information to private parties."

Then I looked up 18 USC 2721 to see what it said about disclosure of personal information from a DMV record. The pertinent section of this law states:

> *Title 18, Sec. 2721. Prohibition on release and use of certain personal information from State motor vehicle records.*
>
> *(b), a State department of motor vehicles, and any officer, employee, or contractor, thereof, shall not knowingly disclose or otherwise make available to any person or entity personal information about any individual obtained by the department in connection with a motor vehicle record.*

There are exceptional cases of disclosure of personal information from DMV records, but these exceptions do not include someone who calls the DMV claiming that you gave them a bad check.

Check Fraud

What does the legitimate merchant do who wants to accept personal checks, but still respects his customers' privacy? How can a merchant protect himself against check fraud without putting his customers at risk of fraud and identity theft themselves?

First, it is necessary to understand that the only way to guarantee you will never receive a bad check is to have a policy of not accepting checks. This may not be such a bad policy in and of itself. If you accept debit cards, which allow your customers to debit money directly from their checking accounts, you provide your customers with much the same convenience of checks without the associated risk. Because debit cards create an electronic debit on their accounts — much like withdrawing money from an ATM — you are assured the money is present at the time of the transaction.

However, there will always be people who want to use checks for direct retail purchases and merchants who are willing to accept them. In this case, there are certain things to be aware of regarding bad checks.

Categories of Bad Checks

First, the majority of checks returned by the bank for insufficient funds are the result of accounting errors on the part of the person writing the check. He failed to balance his checkbook, or made incomplete or inaccurate entries and wrote the check believing there was enough money to cover it. While this type of returned check is certainly an inconvenience for the merchant accepting it, the merchant will usually quickly recover the amount of the check and associated fees.

The next category of "bad checks" comes from individuals who know that there isn't sufficient money in their account to cover the check at the time it is written, but "float" the check, expecting a deposit to arrive and be credited before their checks are processed by the bank. Here too, the merchant accepting such a check will usually recover the amount of the check and associated fees. However, because we are dealing here with more than a simple mistake, it may take a bit more prodding to get the money owed.

Unfortunately, some merchants encourage this type of check fraud by allowing customers to write checks which the merchant agrees to hold until a specific date before depositing or cashing the check. This simply encourages irresponsible use of funds by the customer, and may lead to attempts to "float" checks where merchants have not agreed to hold the check until a future date. Writing a check where one knows there are insufficient funds in the account to cover the check is called "check kiting" and is a misdemeanor in most states. Merchants should not agree to hold checks, thereby participating in this check-kiting scheme and encouraging criminal activity.

Finally, we come to cases of deliberate fraud, where individuals write checks knowing there are insufficient funds to cover them and none will be forthcoming, or write checks on closed accounts. These individuals clearly intend to defraud the merchant accepting the check. Their actions are criminal and can result in significant losses to merchants who are too often stuck with such worthless checks.

Signs of a Bad Check

There are certain indications that a check may be bad. Ninety percent of all bad checks — written knowing that there are insufficient funds to cover the check — are written on fairly new accounts, less than a year old. Low check numbers may indicate these newer accounts. However, a high check number isn't always an indication of a long-established account. Because many printers will let you designate the beginning check sequence number, a new account may have checks beginning with any number. Some banks print the date the account was established on the face of the check. This may read something like "Valued Customer Since 1992." This can help identify a long-established account, but this information can also be inaccurately included by someone having checks printed by someone other than the bank.

The majority of bad checks are passed during the months of October to December. This is likely a result of people spending extra money during the holiday season, relying on holiday bonuses that may be smaller than expected, or simply using bogus checks for holiday purchases and hoping to get away with it.

With the capabilities of desktop publishing, it is possible to print a very convincing check with your home computer and a good-quality printer. Some criminals will simply print up a bunch of checks at home and attempt to cash them. However, these checks usually won't contain the perforations along one edge. Legitimate personal checks and some business checks usually have a perforation along one edge where the check has been torn from the checkbook.

Merchant Protection

If you are going to accept personal checks, in addition to being aware of the signs that indicate a possible bad check, the following steps will help prevent check fraud.

- Checks should be written and signed in front of the person accepting the check. Don't accept a check that has been filled out and signed in advance of making the purchase.
- The person accepting the check should compare the identification of the person preparing the check with the information preprinted on the check itself. For example,

the name and address printed on the check should be an exact match with that on the person's identification.

- The person accepting the check should initial the check above the check number or in another specific location, indicating that he has compared the check with the identification of the person presenting it and it matches.
- Checks for more than the amount of purchase and for more than a given amount should require approval of the store manager or other specific person.
- Checks should be verified whenever possible.

Verification Services

Many banks offer a funds-verification service, allowing one to verify availability of funds in a given checking account. This funds-verification system assists merchants to establish the validity of the check and ensure that funds will be available to cover the amount of the check when it is presented to the bank for processing. In larger banks, the funds-verification system may be totally automated allowing twenty-four hour access. Smaller banks may verify funds only through a teller, thus requiring that any checks be verified during normal banking hours.

I recommend that any merchant accepting personal checks take advantage of the funds-verification system. Depending on the number of personal checks accepted in a day, this may or may not add much of a burden to a business. Generally, however, it is far less burdensome to take the minute or so necessary to verify funds availability on a check than it is to attempt to collect against a check returned for insufficient funds.

To establish a funds-verification system for your business, it is first necessary to contact all of the banks in your area. Ask for and make a list of their funds-verification numbers and the procedure to verify funds on a check. This procedure is normally just a matter of entering the account number, check number, and amount of the check on your touch-tone telephone.

Once you have a list of local banks and their funds-verification numbers, establish a policy for when funds will be verified. The most secure policy is to verify funds on all checks without exception, and to not accept any check where funds cannot be verified. However, if you accept a large number of checks every day, this may be impractical. Therefore, a simple policy such as "funds will be verified on all checks written for more than the amount of purchase and on any check written for $100 or more" will also protect you against many insufficient funds checks.

Using check verification allows a merchant to accept checks without the need to demand that excessive amounts of information be recorded on the check. The merchant could, in fact, accept checks with very limited information about the drafter of the check, because the funds have been verified.

The check-verification procedure is simple, and strongly recommended to all merchants accepting checks as part of their business. However, the procedure is not foolproof. Check verification does not lock funds into the account; it simply verifies that funds are there. A criminal intending to pass several bad checks could write several checks, each for less than the balance of the account, but where the total of all checks written exceeded the balance of the account.

For example, if I know an account contains $100, I can write several checks for $99, all of which will be verified by the check-verification service until the first check actually clears the bank. Thereafter, the check-verification service would not verify checks because of lack of funds and checks that were verified when the account still contained the $100 would be returned for insufficient funds.

In addition to conducting check verification directly with the banks, a merchant may wish to subscribe to one of the major check-verification companies. While there are various check-verification companies in existence, three of the largest are listed here.

ChexSystems: 800-428-9623 or www.chexhelp.com/

SCAN: 877-382-7226 or www.scanassist.com/

TeleCheck: 800-835-3243 or www.telecheck.com/

For a small fee, usually based on the amount of the check being verified, the check-verification companies compare the information you provide with information stored in their databases. If a person has written checks to another merchant using this service, and a check has not been honored, that information will be reported by the check-verification company. This does not prevent the merchant from accepting the check in question, but does warn him that the person presenting the check has written dishonored checks in the past.

There is a constant battle between businesses willing to accept personal checks and criminals who write checks without sufficient funds in their accounts to cover these checks. Add to this, criminals who steal checks and alter them, making victims of both the person from whom the check was stolen and the person accepting the check, and we can see the danger associated with using and accepting checks for direct retail purchases.

Check Acceptance Cards

We have already seen how some merchants demand Social Security numbers, driver's license numbers, and other information be recorded on checks; thereby putting their customers at risk while attempting to protect themselves from receiving a bad check.

A Social Security number does not serve as a means of identification. One may not simply call the Social Security Administration with a given Social Security number and obtain the current name and address of the person to whom the number is assigned. Any merchant that uses Social Security numbers as a way of maintaining its own internal customer database is acting irresponsibly in the extreme.

Driver's license numbers also do little good, as the Driver's Privacy Protection Act prohibits release of information from DMV records for check-verification purposes.

There is, however, a fairly simple way for those merchants willing to accept checks for direct retail purchase to protect themselves without putting their customers at risk. That way is to issue a "Check Acceptance Card" for use when presenting checks to their business.

Customers wishing to use checks for direct retail purchase at a given business are asked to apply for a "Check Acceptance Card" from that business. The customer provides certain identifying information including a telephone number and address. This information is verified by the merchant and the card is then mailed to the customer.

Thereafter, when a customer wants to use a personal check at that business, the person accepting the check need only match the information on the check acceptance card with the check being presented and record the card number on the check itself.

This means that clerks and cashiers are not recording information on customers' checks that does little but invade the customers' privacy. Customers do not have to worry about crimes like identity theft because they preprinted excessive amounts of information on their checks. However, if a customer does have a check returned, for whatever reason, business management has contact information for that individual on file to aid in collection of funds.

While perhaps not the perfect solution, check acceptance cards provide protection for both the customer and the merchant. It is a system which is easy to implement, and where it has been used, the number of checks returned as unpaid by the bank and uncollected from the customer dropped to almost zero.

Check Alteration

Another type of fraud associated with checks is alteration of a legitimate check, making it payable to someone other than the intended recipient, or altering the amount of the check, making it payable for more than intended.

This alteration of checks is a simple matter when the person drafting the check does not completely fill in all required information or leaves blank space before or after information entered onto the check. This is commonly seen where a person will draft a check and leave the "Pay to the order of" line blank, intending that the person receiving the check will fill it in or that a business will have a stamp for that line of the check.

Merchants should not use a stamp for the "pay-to" line of a check. Customers should be required to make the check payable to the merchant. Simply having a sign posted at the check-out area detailing the merchant's check acceptance policy and telling them who to make checks payable to, will make this a simple matter for customers. Likewise, if you cash checks as a service to your customers, you should never accept a check with a blank "pay-to" line, or a check that has been altered in any way. This includes checks where the "pay-to" line has been filled in by someone other than the drafter of the check.

Check-Washing

Check alteration is a serious crime which results in losses of $815 million every year in the United States, and this sum is increasing steadily. However, these losses are not just from alteration of improperly drafted checks, but from a procedure known as "check washing," where the information written on a check is erased by a criminal and replaced with information allowing the criminal to cash the check.

When most of us write a check, we fill out the required information with whatever ink pen we have handy and then send the check off to pay whomever. Criminals obtain these checks, often by stealing them from the mail, and then wash out the information written on the check, altering it to meet the criminal's needs.

Chemicals that can be used to wash out the printed information on a check include such common chemicals as acetone, carbon tetrachloride, or simple household bleach. Washing out the information on a check using these chemicals takes a little bit of experimenting to get it right, but is actually fairly easy once you get the hang of it. While writing this chapter, I tried washing the information off some of my own checks. After a little practice, I found I could wash out and alter a check in a very short time. (I have since changed to checks with security features to prevent check washing.)

The National Check Fraud Center's Web site, www.ckfraud.org/washing.html, tells of one woman who became very proficient at this criminal activity, ...she prowled the streets with a portable computer, printer and laminating machine in her car, cranking out new identification each time she swiped a batch of bills. Of course she had to take the time to wash the ink from the two vital areas of the check, making sure she didn't tamper with the written signature.

Check-Washing Scenario

How does a check-washing scheme work? First, our check-washing criminal comes up with some type of identification that can be used when cashing the altered checks. This can be a fake ID of some type or a stolen ID where the person that will be cashing the checks fits the basic description on the ID. Most people checking ID just match names anyway, and ID photos are generally poor, so any reasonable likeness will work.

Next, our check-washing criminal steals a number of checks from outgoing mail focusing on the envelopes that are used to pay bills, which are usually paid by check. This is not a difficult problem in areas where people tend to place mail in their home mailbox to be picked up by the mailman when he delivers mail for the day. This check stealing can go on over a period of a couple weeks before anyone is even likely to notice.

The checks are washed and altered to be made payable to the person represented by the fake or stolen ID. Checks for fairly large amounts — such as car payments or rent — may only have the "pay-to" line altered. Checks for smaller amounts may have the amount altered also. These criminals don't care if the check bounces, but they want to be sure that if the place cashing the check uses a check-verification service, there will be sufficient money in the account to cover the check. On the other hand, if the criminals know that the place cashing the checks doesn't verify the checks, they may just alter the amount to whatever they think they can get away with.

In a large city there are various places other than a bank, where one may cash a check. The check-washing criminals will certainly have located a number of these places before they begin stealing checks. Imagine that during the period of one month a criminal steals one hundred checks. He then washes the checks and after altering them, is able to cash them for an average of $500 each. Remember that rent checks and the like may already be made out for more than this. During this one-month period, the criminal would get away with $50,000. A well-organized check-washing ring will likely be able to do much better than this.

If criminals are able to avoid altering the amount of the checks, the drafters of the checks will not even immediately notice that the check is stolen. They send off the payment and the check clears the bank. The drafter of the check will likely assume that it was received and cashed by the person or business to whom he originally sent it. Businesses not receiving a payment do little more than send notice of the missed payment with the following month's billing. Checks that have the amount of the check altered in addition to the pay-to line may bounce or cause other checks written on the account to bounce, but check-washing criminals have at least a few weeks of operating time before there is likely to be a specific investigative effort. It will take a number of checks on a number of accounts being detected as altered checks before there will be a concerted effort by law enforcement against these criminals. Furthermore, the criminals face very little risk of getting caught in this crime. Even if one of the places where they attempt to cash the altered checks questions them, they need only try someplace else.

Prevention

To protect yourself against this type of criminal, it is essential that you protect your checks from falling into their hands. This means not placing outgoing mail in your home mailbox where it can be stolen. Take mail to the post office or actually hand it to the mailman when he comes to your home to deliver the daily mail.

If you have a home business or are otherwise in a position to receive checks from others, be sure to protect those incoming checks from theft, too. Receiving mail at a post office box is perhaps the most secure way, but if you receive mail at home or a business, be sure that the mail is picked up as soon as it is delivered or that it is placed in a locked mailbox. Mail thieves often follow closely behind the mailman, stealing the mail within fifteen minutes after it has been delivered.

If you receive mail along a rural delivery route, or if your mailbox is at the end of your driveway or in a cluster along the road, you may want to consider installing a locking mailbox. One simple way to do this is to attach a padlock to your mailbox, leaving it unlocked and inside the mailbox. When the mailman delivers your mail he removes the padlock, places your mail in the box, and snaps the lock shut through the door and body of the mailbox. Most street-side mailboxes already have these holes in place to allow the box to be locked with a padlock. If you use a lock on your mailbox, however, it is important to remember to pick up your mail every day. The mailman won't be able to deliver mail to your box if it is still locked when he arrives the next day.

In addition to protecting incoming and outgoing checks, it is also important to protect your supply of blank checks. Someone stealing your blank checks can accomplish check forgery just as easily as they can wash checks that have already been filled out. Safeguard your checkbook and supply of blank checks. When you order a new supply of checks, pay close attention to the expected arrival date of the package and notify your bank if you don't receive it when expected.

Finally, order checks that contain special security features, such as anti-washing paper that reacts with the chemicals commonly used to wash checks, making the check itself useless, if someone washes it.

Using Checks Safely

Checks are a convenient tool, but it is important to use them safely. Use them only to pay established accounts or for purchases conducted through the mail. Checks should never be used to make a direct retail purchase: that is, you write a check at a store, hand it to the cashier, and leave with your purchases. Along this same line, I recommend that merchants, as a general business practice, not accept checks for direct retail purchase. With the current trend toward a cashless society, almost any place where one could write a personal check, one could also use a credit card or debit card.

From an anti-fraud/anti-identity-theft viewpoint, your personal checks should contain very little personal information. We have already seen that checks should not have such things as driver's license or Social Security numbers printed on them, but you may also want to consider removing your address and telephone number from your checks.

For many years I have maintained a checking account with my name as the only personal information preprinted on my checks. I use my checks to pay recurring debts where I have an established account like telephone bills and automobile insurance. The lack of preprinted personal information on my checks has never caused any question or delay in service. When I pay a bill with a check containing no personal information, it is processed in the same manner as a check that contains multiple lines of personal information and cross-referenced identification numbers: it is deposited by the business receiving the check and clears my bank normally.

On rare occasions, I have also made a retail purchase of items through the mail and paid with a check. Again, the only personal information on my check is my name. When a retailer accepts personal checks for mail-order purchases, he will either ship the ordered items immediately upon processing the order or, more likely, will hold the order until personal checks have been cleared by the bank. If a merchant has a policy of holding orders until personal checks clear the bank, it makes no difference how much or how little personal information is on the check; it will be held until it clears. If the merchant immediately ships orders that are paid for by personal check, the amount of personal information on your check again makes no difference. Orders are processed based on information contained on the order form, not on the face of your check.

The merchant who accepts personal checks for mail-order purchases, and holds shipment of the order until the check clears, takes no risk. He maintains possession of his products until checks clear. For service accounts, if a check fails to clear the bank, the service provider can simply terminate the service. The lack of personal information preprinted on the face of your check is immaterial. Service accounts are already going to have information about you in their records. The telephone company does not need to look on the face of your check to determine your mailing address and telephone number.

Another way to limit personal information on your checks is, if it is not preprinted on the check, don't write it in by hand. If you are paying your telephone bill with a personal check, don't write your telephone number on the check. Almost all bills and invoices include a portion to be returned with payment. This is the item used by the payment processor to ensure that it is credited to the correct account. Of course, the person processing payments will look at the check to ensure that he credits the correct amount paid, but is probably not paying close attention to other notations on the check, nor is he updating address and telephone information on your account with information preprinted on your check.

Simply put, there is no need to have extensive personal information preprinted on your checks. It is only when trying to use checks for direct purchase, where you do not have an established account, that the business accepting your check will want you to include personal information on the face of your check.

Chapter Three
Credit Cards

Using a major credit card provides the user with a great
deal of convenience and some degree of protection in making purchases. The convenience of credit cards needs little
explanation, but the protection provided when using a credit
card is something that we should take time to look at.

Customer Liability

With a credit card, you can make large purchases without
carrying large amounts of cash. You can make a $1,000 pur-
chase without the need to carry that much cash. If you lose
cash, it is generally gone forever; however, if you lose your
credit card, you have good protection under federal law and
under the policies of the credit card companies themselves.

If you have properly signed your credit card and it is lost
or stolen and ends up being used by someone to make purchases that you never authorized, you are not liable for those
charges. Federal law (The Fair Credit Billing Act) provides
that you are liable for only fifty dollars as a result of fraudu-

lent charges on your credit card if you report this to your credit card company immediately upon discovery. Both MasterCard and VISA have a "zero liability" policy by which they absorb even this fifty dollars if you are the victim of a crime involving the misuse of your credit cards.

Another advantage of using a credit card for direct retail purchase is that, while it gives you a record of your transaction, you can still maintain a good degree of privacy, because the merchant has no information about you other than your name in association with the purchase.

Demands for Personal Information

Unfortunately, there is a growing trend among certain unscrupulous merchants of demanding supplementary information and identification from customers using a properly signed credit card to make their purchases. This demand for supplementary identification violates the policies of the credit card companies and their merchant agreements with those businesses accepting credit cards. Presenting supplementary identification when using a credit card simply puts the cardholder at risk of identity theft and other associated crimes, while providing the cardholder with no additional protection against fraud.

When a merchant demanding supplementary identification from a cardholder is asked why it is necessary, some of these merchants will state that the credit card companies require them to obtain additional identification from cardholders, even when their credit card is properly signed. This is a lie. Consider the following policy statements regarding requests for supplementary information by merchants as a condition of making a purchase with a credit card:

> Please be assured that merchants may not refuse to honor a Visa card simply because the cardholder refuses a request for supplementary information. The only exception is when a Visa card is unsigned when presented. In this situation, a merchant must obtain authorization, review additional identification, and require the cardholder to sign the card before completing a transaction. — VISA International, Owings Mills, MD 21117

> The merchant cannot require additional identification as a standard business practice when you use MasterCard for payment. There are a few exceptions, such as when additional information is required to complete the transaction. For example, a merchant will need your address if goods are to be delivered to your home. — MasterCard International, St. Louis, MO 63146

Other merchants will tell you that they demand additional identification from their customers in order to protect the customer from having to pay thousands of dollars in fraudulent charges if someone has stolen the customer's credit card and is using it to make purchases in his name. This claim also fails, since under federal law the maximum liability to the cardholder is fifty dollars, and the credit card companies waive this fee anyway with their "zero liability" policies.

In fact, the credit card companies are so concerned about these demands for supplementary information as a condition to making a purchase with a properly signed credit card, that they encourage cardholders to report these violations to them. Merchants who repeatedly violate their contractual agreements with the credit card companies may have their ability to accept credit cards revoked. If you are faced with demands for supplementary identification when using your properly signed credit card, you should make it a point to report these violations to the credit card company. This can be done by calling the number on your credit card or by contacting the customer relations departments of the credit card companies directly.

Visa USA
Consumer Relations
PO Box 8999
San Francisco, CA 94128

MasterCard International
Public Relations
2000 Purchase Street
Purchase, NY 10577

American Express
Customer Service
PO Box 297812
Ft. Lauderdale, Fl 33329-7812

"See ID"

In addition to these inappropriate demands for supplementary identification by merchants, we are starting to see some cardholders write things like "See ID" or "Check ID" in place of their signature on the back of their credit cards. These people mistakenly believe that this somehow protects them from fraud or forgery if someone steals their credit card. Unfortunately, just the opposite is true. An unsigned credit card or one containing words such as "Check ID" in place of the authorizing signature, actually makes it easier to use the card fraudulently if it is lost or stolen.

The credit card companies are billion-dollar companies with extensive anti-fraud and security departments. Consider what they have determined regarding these "Check ID" schemes. The following VISA anti-fraud training script is available on the VISA Web site.

VISA Merchant Fraud Awareness Training Script

- Remember, a Visa card is not valid unless it is signed by the cardholder. Unfortunately, there are some cardholders who think an unsigned card, or one with "Check ID" written in the signature panel is more secure. This is not true — it just allows criminals to sign the card, or use a fake ID with their signature.
- What if the signature panel instructs the merchant to "Check ID?" A card where the customer has written "Check ID" in the signature panel is considered an unsigned card.
- NOTE: Effective January 1, 1998, the words "Not Valid Unless Signed" are printed near the signature panel on all Visa cards. This requirement provides merchants with an independent source to refer to when requesting that cardholders sign their cards, as well as justification for refusing to accept an unsigned card.

There is also a concept in the law called "due diligence." *Black's Law Dictionary* (6th ed.), defines this as: Such a measure of prudence, activity, or assiduity, as is properly to be expected from, and ordinarily exercised by, a reasonable and prudent man under the particular circumstances; not measured by any absolute standard, but depending on the relative facts of the special case.

This is a lawyer's way of saying that one must take reasonable care to protect oneself from harm or like adverse effect. Federal law limits a cardholder's liability to fifty dollars and the credit card companies have gone one step further and granted a zero liability to card holders in cases where their card is lost or stolen and used without their permission. However, it may be rightly argued that a cardholder must exercise due diligence in preventing the unauthorized use of his credit card.

The credit card companies require that a cardholder immediately sign his credit card with an authorizing signature as soon as he receives the card, and certainly before he starts carrying it around and attempts to use it to make purchases.

A cardholder who does not sign his credit card or writes "See ID" in place of the authorizing signature, is not acting with reasonable care. In fact, such action is clearly negligent and may possibly waive the cardholder's limited liability under the law. Any cardholder who fails to sign his credit card, or who uses words like "See ID" in place of the authorizing signature, and any merchant who accepts a card so annotated, should be held liable for 100 percent of any fraudulent charges made against the card if it is ever lost or stolen.

So what is behind demands for supplementary identification and "Check ID" in place of signatures? It seems fairly clear that this violates the policy of the credit card companies and actually puts cardholders at risk. In a very small percentage of cases, the merchant demanding photo ID when you attempt to pay for dinner with your credit card may think he is actually helping prevent misuse of the credit card and protecting his customers. However, in the vast majority of cases, when a merchant demands some type of supplementary identification as a condition of using a properly signed credit card, there is something else involved.

Why Merchants Demand Supplementary Information

Demands for supplementary identification are often part of a business's marketing plan. If you disclose information about yourself to the merchant, you may find that you are soon receiving a flood of advertising from this merchant and from everyone to whom he has sold or rented his customer lists. One major chain of stores selling radios and electronics routinely asks customers to disclose their name, address, and telephone number, even if the customer is paying with cash.

On the other hand, demands for supplementary identification may be part of a credit card fraud or identity theft scheme on the part of an unscrupulous merchant. Remember, although hackers stealing credit card numbers from a computer database make the news, most credit card fraud results from credit card numbers and supplementary identification being misused by someone who has obtained that information during the course of a legitimate business transaction.

Furthermore, there may be other criminal intent involved when a clerk at some shop demands ID when you present your credit card for payment. Most people who are faced with a demand for ID will present their driver's license. A driver's license contains your address on its face, thus letting the person seeing it know where you live.

An underpaid clerk demanding ID from you when you purchase that new stereo may think that he and a couple of his friends can drop by your home when you are away and add it to their own collection. Maybe these criminals have something else in mind for the young woman who presents her driver's license — and home address — as a condition of using her credit card.

You should understand that there is no requirement for you to provide any type of supplementary information when using your properly signed credit card to make a purchase. Any merchant who requests that you present ID along with your credit card is acting in violation of his merchant's agreement with the credit card companies, and is putting you at risk of identity theft, credit card fraud, and other crimes.

Protecting Your Credit Card

Here is a list of simple precautions you can take to avoid becoming a victim of credit card fraud.

- Make sure that your credit cards are all properly signed with an authorizing signature. Don't use such things as "Check ID" in place of your signature. If you have something in place of your signature now, get your credit cards replaced and sign them properly.

- If a merchant makes a demand for "photo ID" or other supplementary information as a condition of using your credit card, you must always refuse to provide that information. Additionally, whether you are able to complete the transaction without providing the supplementary information or not, you should report the merchant's inappropriate conduct to your credit card company.

- If it seems that the merchant actually believes that he is protecting his customers with these demands for ID, explain to the merchant that neither VISA nor MasterCard require you to present supplementary information as a condition of using your credit card. Speak with the business's manager and ask for a clarification of their policy in this matter.

- If you can't resolve this matter with the merchant, take your business elsewhere. You should never have to conduct business with anyone who maintains a policy that clearly puts his customers at risk.

Credit Card Fraud

If you are a merchant and you accept credit cards, you will increase your business potential, but you also face certain risks from credit card fraud. For our purposes, we will define credit card fraud as purchases made — or attempted — using a credit card as the method of payment where said payment was not authorized by the legitimate holder of the credit card. These purchases and attempts may be made in person, or over the telephone or Internet, where information is provided from the credit card, but the purchaser and credit card are not physically present at the point of sale.

Don't Be A Victim!
How to Protect Yourself from Hoaxes, Scams, and Frauds

58

First, look at fraud attempts where the credit card is present. In these cases the criminal attempting the credit card fraud has found or stolen the credit card in question and is attempting to make purchases with the card before its legitimate holder can report it missing. This can be a nuisance for the cardholder, but the law limits cardholder liability in these cases to fifty dollars, and both MasterCard and VISA have a zero-liability policy where they waive this fifty-dollar liability for their cardholders.

Merchant Liability

A merchant making a sale to someone using a stolen credit card becomes liable for the cost of the merchandise or service provided to the criminal. To combat this fraud, some banks give cardholders the option of having their photograph added to their credit card. This is a reasonable security precaution, but the photographs are generally of poor quality. So while this may prevent a twenty-three-year old black female from passing herself off as a sixty-three-year old white male, someone of the same general appearance as the legitimate cardholder will probably be able to use it.

Some merchants and cardholders believe that requiring supplementary identification to be presented with the credit card will prevent use of stolen credit cards. Unfortunately, demands for supplementary identification and "See ID" instructions in place of an authorizing signature actually make credit card fraud easier, and put cardholders at greater risk of credit card fraud and identity theft. The major credit card companies recognize this and prohibit demands for supplementary information as a condition of making a purchase with a credit card.

The risk of this practice comes from the fact that most credit card fraud does not involve use of the actual credit card, but rather the information from that card: credit card number, expiration date, cardholder's name, and any supplementary information the criminal may have been able to obtain. While stories of hackers breaking into computer databases and stealing thousands of credit card numbers certainly make the news, most credit card numbers are stolen the old-fashioned way, by unscrupulous retailers who make duplicate copies of charge slips or scan the information stored on the magnetic strip into a hand-held reader. The last thing you want to do, as a cardholder, is provide supplementary information to the single greatest source of stolen credit card numbers — the merchant.

Merchant Security

As a merchant, demanding supplementary identification from your customers does little to protect you or your customers, and it violates your merchant's agreement with the credit card companies. However, you should not just blindly accept any credit card handed to you for payment. Instead, follow the security checks established by the credit card companies, which protect you and your customers from fraud.

- Never accept an unsigned credit card.

- Never accept a credit card with "See ID" or similar words in place of a signature. The credit card companies consider this to be an unsigned card.

- Look at the name on the credit card. Is a man presenting a card in the name of Suzie Jones, or a woman presenting a card in the name of John Smith?

- Hold the card throughout the transaction and compare the signature on the back of the card with the signature on the charge slip.

- Obtain authorization, either by an electronic card reader or calling to receive an authorization number. Don't accept a card that cannot be authorized.

Telephone and Online Purchases

A question that often comes up when discussing online purchases is: "Just how safe is it to enter my credit card number online to make a purchase from a Web site?" If you are dealing with an established business and the Web site is using Secure Socket Layer (SSL) to transmit order information, the actual online transaction is very safe. The online order is much more secure than handing your credit card to a store clerk or waitress working for minimum wage and tips. The online transaction is encrypted with a strong algorithm. The credit card in the hands of a merchant has no such protection. Any threat of loss of your credit card number from an online purchase comes from the way it is handled by the merchant who receives it, not from the possibility that some super hacker will be able to break SSL encryption protocols just to steal your credit card number.

As a merchant, however, you face the possibility that the person placing an order from your Web site or over the telephone is not an authorized user of the credit card to which you will be billing the transaction. The card is not physically presented during the transaction and you have no signature to compare to the authorizing signature on the credit card itself. If you ship merchandise to someone who uses stolen credit card information, you will be out the cost of the merchandise when the legitimate cardholder demands a refund of the money billed fraudulently to his card and his bank issues a charge-back against your merchant account. Furthermore, you will also be charged a fee because of this charge-back. So it pays to take steps to ensure that the person charging a purchase to a credit card is actually an authorized user of the card in question.

You have already seen that much credit card fraud does not involve possession of the actual credit card. When a legitimate cardholder loses his credit card or has it stolen, he usually quickly reports this to the card issuer, who in turn quickly cancels the account. However, if a criminal has simply obtained the card data, the legitimate cardholder may not even be aware of it until he discovers unauthorized charges on his credit card bill.

CVV2 or CVC2

The first step in preventing online and telephonic credit card fraud is to determine that the person placing the order actually is in possession of the credit card. The credit card companies have established a way to do this by including a verification number, printed on credit cards, which is not part of the account number. This number is known as CVV2 or CVC2 (Card Verification Value/Code 2). The CVV2/CVC2 is a three-digit number printed after the card number in the signature panel on the back of the credit card.

The CVV2/CVC2 is calculated using a proprietary algorithm based on account data from the card, and cannot be determined simply by knowing the credit card number. Your merchant credit card verification system can be set to perform a check on the CVV2/CVC2. By asking for the CVV2/CVC2 as part of the transaction information during an online/telephone order and verifying this number as part of your merchant credit card verification process, you can determine that the person placing the order is in possession of the credit card. It is possible that a criminal could have copied the CVV2/CVC2 from the card, but remember, lost and stolen cards tend to get reported. Furthermore, if the criminal stealing credit card data is doing so from a source other than the credit card itself, the CVV2/CVC2 will likely not be present.

You can also ask a customer to identify the bank issuing the credit card. You can then confirm that the first six numbers of the credit card are those assigned to that bank. This requires that you call your merchant account and have them verify this information for you.

Address Verification

The next step in ensuring that the person placing an online or telephone order is authorized to charge to that credit card number is to use the address verification system. The address verification system compares the billing address a cardholder has on file with his bank with the address provided during the online or telephone order. The address verification system actually compares the numeric portions of the address and zip code on file with the information you enter. For example, if you are provided with an address for Max Rogers,

123 Rodeo Drive, Beverly Hills, CA 90210, the address will compare the numbers "123" and the zip code "90210," attempting to match this with information on file with the cardholder's bank.

Of course, a criminal certainly could obtain the billing address of the credit card number he has stolen. In this case, the criminal would present the correct billing information, but would have the product shipped elsewhere. This is another very important reason not to present supplementary identification when using your credit card in person. This only gives a criminal more information to steal your credit and identity.

The address verification system is valid only for addresses in the United States. If you take international orders this security check will be unavailable to you. However, it certainly pays to use the address verification system on all orders within the United States. It isn't perfect, but it adds a security check to your online and telephone orders that helps reduce fraud. In addition to saving you the cost of products lost to fraud and the associated charge-back fees, using the address verification system may qualify you for lower rates on your merchant account.

Detecting a Fraudulent Order

In addition to using CVV2/CVC2 and address verification, anyone processing online or telephone orders should review orders as they are processed. These questions can help to detect fraudulent orders or to verify that an order being placed is valid.

- Is a repeat customer placing the order? An order being placed in the name of someone who has ordered from your company before, and being shipped to an address where you have shipped previous orders, is likely to be a valid order.

- Is the order unusual when compared to other orders placed with your business? For example, if the average online or telephone order is for $50-$100, and you receive an order for $700, this would be unusual.

- Does the person placing the order request that it be sent by express or overnight delivery? A criminal engaged in credit card fraud doesn't care about the extra cost for these services, since he isn't going to pay the bill anyway.

- Are the billing and ship-to addresses different? A criminal may have been able to determine the billing address of a person's credit card, but he will not have the items ordered on a stolen credit card sent to the legitimate holder of the card.

- Is an online order being placed using one of the many free e-mail services, such as Hotmail or Yahoo? Many people establish a free account to use for conducting business online. This is normally done to help limit the amount of spam received at their paid account. However, the majority of legitimate users of free e-mail services also have a "paid account." Request that customers provide a valid e-mail address from a paid ISP where you can send an e-mail verification of the order. Send an e-mail confirming the order, but never send advertising or other information to a customer's e-mail address unless he has specifically requested that he receive additional e-mail from your business.

There are times when even a legitimate order may raise a warning flag. The address-verification system may not match if a cardholder has recently moved but not yet updated his address information with his credit card company or bank. A new customer may find that you sell exactly what he has been looking for and place a larger-than-normal order, but this certainly will be the exception to the rule. In a case where these warning signs are present, it may be advisable to conduct additional follow-up checks before accepting the order, and in some cases even refuse an order.

Verified By VISA

An excellent program to combat online credit card fraud has been established by VISA. This program, called "Verified By VISA," allows you to attach a security code or PIN to your VISA cards for use while shopping online.

The Verified By VISA program works like this: Using your existing VISA card, you log onto the VISA Web site at www.visa.com and follow the links to the Verified By VISA page. You then register your VISA card numbers and choose a security code/PIN to be used with that number when shopping online with participating merchants. Thereafter, when you use your VISA card to shop online with a participating merchant, the credit card verification system recognizes that you have registered your VISA card in the Verified By VISA system and will require that you enter your security code/PIN to authorize the transaction. For merchants not participating in the Verified By VISA program, your VISA card works normally without requiring you to enter the authorizing security code.

The Verified By VISA program is an excellent security program with great potential to reduce online credit card fraud. It allows VISA cardholders to add additional security to their cards without it being burdensome or invasive of personal privacy. The downside is that it is still (at the time of this writing) a fairly new program and has a limited number of participating merchants and VISA issuing banks. However, many merchants are already participating in the Verified By VISA program, and more are added on a regular basis. If you use your VISA card to shop online, or if you are a merchant accepting online payments, it is a good idea to sign up for the Verified By VISA program.

Opt-Out — Financial Services Modernization Act (Gramm-Leach-Bliley Act)

Many financial service organizations — credit card companies, banks, investment firms, etc. — sell personally identifiable information about you to other companies and individuals. This includes companies with which they may be affiliated and various third-party companies with which they have no direct affiliation. The reason they do this is that your personally identifiable information and credit worthiness data is worth money to companies wanting to market their products and services to you.

Do you receive preapproved credit offers? Do you receive mortgage offers and offers for preapproved loans? If you do, it is likely that information about you and your credit worthiness was provided by a financial service organization with which you currently conduct business.

Several problems arise with this, not the least of which is that these preapproved offers for credit, loans, or whatever greatly increase the possibility of you becoming a victim of identity theft if you don't carefully destroy the applications you receive. Furthermore, the financial institutions selling your personally identifiable information are demonstrating a complete disregard for your personal privacy and the privacy of your financial information. This complete disregard for the privacy of their customers by many financial organizations is so pervasive and offensive that the federal government finally had to establish laws to allow individuals the right to prohibit this wanton disclosure of their private information.

Sometime in the spring or early summer of 2001, you received a notice from your various financial service organizations telling you that you had the right to opt-out of their selling your private information. Most likely this notice was included with one of your monthly statements, along with a flier advertising rates on new car loans and an offer for a free pen and pencil set. Many people missed this notice or did not understand what it meant.

In short, what these notices said was that you had until July 1, 2001, to inform your various financial service organizations that you did not want them to sell your personally identifiable information and information about your credit worthincss, or they were free to continue doing so.

Opting Out Process

Fortunately, the Financial Services Modernization Act allows you to opt-out of this sale of your information at any time. If you didn't opt-out prior to July 1, 2001, your finan cial service organizations may be selling your information, but you can stop them from doing so now. The following sample letter can be used to protect your privacy and stop your financial organizations from selling information about you. Simply send a copy of this letter — adjusted as necessary to meet your personal requirements — to all of your financial organizations. The letter should be dated and signed, and should include your name, address, and account number and the name and address of the financial institution.

[Date]

[Your Name]
[Your Address]

[Financial Institution Name]
[Financial Institution Address]

Re: Opt-Out Instructions for Account # [Your Account Number]

Dear Sir or Madam:

This letter contains my instructions with regard to your information sharing and sales policies:

You may NOT share my personally identifiable information with nonaffiliated third-party companies or individuals.

You may NOT share nonpublic personal information about me with affiliated companies or individuals.

I am asserting my rights under the Financial Services Modernization Act (the Gramm-Leach-Bliley Act) to opt-out of any sharing or sales of my information by your company.

You may NOT share information about my credit worthiness with any affiliate of your company.

I am asserting my rights under the Fair Credit Reporting Act to opt-out of any sharing of this information by your company.

I do not wish to receive marketing offers from your company or its affiliates. Please delete my name from all of your marketing lists and databases.

Your privacy notice states you may otherwise use my information as "permitted by law." I wish to limit other uses of my personal information by your company and its affiliates. In particular:

You may NOT disclose any information about me, including transaction and experience information, to your affiliates.

You may NOT disclose any information about me in connection with direct marketing agreements between your company and another company.

Thank you for respecting my privacy and honoring my choices regarding my customer information.

Please acknowledge your intention to comply with my request for privacy of my personal financial and other information.

Sincerely,

[Your Signature]
[Your Name]

Credit Reporting Agency Prescreening

In addition to contacting the individual financial organizations with which you deal and instructing them not to disclose your personal information, you should also instruct the major credit reporting agencies — Equifax, Experian, and TransUnion — not to disclose your personal information as part of prescreened credit offers.

If you receive preapproved offers for credit cards, loans, and lines of credit, it is likely that this preapproval came about because the major credit reporting agencies are selling information about your creditworthiness. They are selling your private financial information without your permission and without giving you any notice that they have done so, or to whom they have sold information about you. You can, of course, write to each of the credit reporting agencies and instruct them not to disclose your personal information, but in the case of Equifax, Experian, and TransUnion, you can also opt-out by calling 1-888-5-OPTOUT (1-888-567-8688).

When you call the opt-out number, you will be asked to leave the following personal information, to allow the credit reporting agencies to properly identify you and remove you from their prescreening lists:

- Home telephone number
- Name
- Zip code
- Street address
- Social Security number

The information you provide is considered confidential by the credit reporting agencies and is used only for the purpose of removing your name from the prescreening lists. You will have the option of removing your name from these prescreening lists for two years, or removing your name from these lists permanently. I recommend that you choose the permanent removal option.

Having your name removed from the prescreening lists does not adversely affect your ability to apply for credit or loans and authorize a company to screen your records for that purpose. It does, however, stop the flood of preapproved "junk mail" offers which you must make a point to destroy, or risk them being used by someone targeting you for fraud or identity theft.

Direct Marketing Association Opt-Out

While we are working on our opt-out requests, it will be beneficial to send opt-out letters to the Direct Marketing Association. The Direct Marketing Association, as their name implies, supports direct marketing through mass-mailing and telemarketing calls. However, they realize that not everyone is interested in receiving this advertising. Therefore, the Direct Marketing Association maintains a Mail Preference Service and a Telephone Preference Service allowing you to request that your name, address, and telephone number be removed from direct marketing lists. These are free services and actually help to reduce junk mail and telemarketing calls from legitimate businesses that subscribe to the Direct Marketing Associations "opt-out lists."

To have your name removed from many direct marketing lists, send a request to the Mail Preference Service and Telephone Preference Service at the following addresses. The Direct Marketing Association distributes their updated list quarterly, so you should begin to see a reduction in the amount of junk mail in your mailbox and a decrease in telemarketing calls about three months after you send in your opt-out request. The Direct Marketing Association also maintains an e-mail advertising opt-out list to which you may wish to add your e-mail address. This can be done at their Web site: www.the-dma.org.

Mail Preference Service
Direct Marketing Association
PO Box 3079
Grand Central Station, NY 10163

Telephone Preference Service
Direct Marketing Association
PO Box 3079
Grand Central Station, NY 10163

You may wonder why it is important to opt-out of direct marketing mail and telemarketing offers as a way to safeguard yourself against hoaxes, scams, and frauds. The reason for this is actually quite simple: To be targeted as a victim of a hoax, scam, fraud, or identity theft, the criminal must first obtain some degree of information about you. Although a "legitimate" business using direct mail for advertising and special offers may pose little criminal threat to you, a criminal who steals your mail can use special offers and advertising sent to you as a starting point for criminal activity targeting you. You may, of course, simply shred all the junk mail that you receive and pay to have it hauled away as trash, but unless you are responding to a majority of the advertisements you receive in the mail, it is better to opt-out. You can always request information from a company with which you choose to deal.

When it comes to telemarketing, we will see in Chapter Five that even legitimate telemarketers can pose a very real threat to your privacy and personal safety. Likewise, we have seen that unsolicited commercial e-mail (spam) is almost always a scam. Quality businesses simply don't flood your e-mail account with unsolicited e-mail, costing you money, time, and computer storage space.

Any minimal advantage you may receive from direct marketing offers is greatly outweighed by the potential harm you can suffer should criminals take advantage of this route to target you for hoaxes, scams, frauds, and identity theft. Therefore, opt-out.

Chapter Four
Identity Theft

Identity theft is one of the fastest growing crimes in America today. Government reports indicate that 500,000 people per year are victims of identity theft, and that number is continuing to grow. Advancing technology and the development of a cashless society make identity theft both an easy and profitable crime to commit and one in which the likelihood of being caught is fairly slim. Perhaps the greatest contributing factor to the crime of identity theft is the use of universal identification numbers — such as your Social Security number — and the cross-referencing of accounts and databases by these numbers. A thief who gains access to one of your accounts or personal information contained in some database, now has access to many additional accounts and sources of information about you.

Identity theft takes two basic forms. The first is where a thief makes a complete assumption of your identity. He takes any information he can learn about you and incorporates it into his new identity, using it to "become" you. The second form of identity theft is where a thief uses just parts of your identity to give an appearance of legitimacy to his criminal activity.

Whether the identity thief steals your identity and begins living his life using your personal identifying information, or simply uses part of your identity in the furtherance of a crime, it will, at the least, cause you to expend significant time and effort to clear up the problems caused by this identity thief. More likely, however, is that there will be permanent damage to your reputation, credit rating, and personal sense of safety.

How to Steal Someone's Identity

Stealing someone's identity is not all that difficult. In fact, anyone can steal the identity of the average person who takes no precautions to protect himself against this type of crime. To steal someone's identity, you need to know a little bit about that person. Of course, you will want to know the name of the person and probably the date and place of his birth. Other information, such as current address, account numbers for various accounts, and employer, also come in handy.

Then you need the one key that makes identity theft so easy — that person's Social Security number. The Social Security number has become a national identification number, tying together numerous individual accounts and information in multiple databases. Once you learn someone's Social Security number, you have the key to accessing multiple accounts and sources of personal and private information.

So, you know the following information about your intended victim: name, address, Social Security number, date and place of birth, and current bank account number or credit card number.

You may have noticed that much of this information is often recorded on personal checks. Remember our unscrupulous merchants and their demands for unnecessary information on checks, and their demands for ID when you attempt to use a credit card? If you could steal our victim's wallet or purse, or even get access to it long enough to copy information from its contents, you would have a great deal of the information you need to steal this person's identity. However, it's not absolutely necessary to steal a wallet or purse, or even to come into contact with your victim.

Because of the ever-increasing demands that we disclose extensive amounts of personal information for such simple acts as renting a video or obtaining a library card, an identity thief may be able to gain access to significant amounts of information about an individual with very little effort. Do you think that there is any security provided for the customer database at your local video store? Is the public library storing patron information in encrypted databases? Think about the information demanded from you on a regular basis and just how much damage could be done with that information in the hands of an identity thief.

Establishing the Stolen Identity

First, you need to produce a fake identification card using the personal information of your victim. With the current capabilities of desktop publishing, this is not too difficult. The fake ID should be of good quality, but it need not be perfect for these purposes. There are driver's license templates from all fifty states available on the Internet, allowing

Don't Be A Victim!
How to Protect Yourself from Hoaxes, Scams, and Frauds

76

you to produce valid-looking driver's licenses and IDs. Additionally, there are various places where you can buy "novelty" ID, filled in with any information you want.

The trick here is to produce a driver's license or ID card that is not local to where you will use it. If you are going to assume an identity stolen from Oregon, use that identity in a distant state, for example, Virginia. Someone from Oregon will probably know what a Oregon driver's license looks like, but someone from Virginia will probably have no idea what an Oregon driver's license looks like. (Yes, I just moved here from Oregon. I really like it here. Got to get my license changed to Virginia next week.) If you have done your homework, you know the actual state of issue and driver's license number of the person whose identity you are stealing.

A state Department of Motor Vehicles (DMV) is prohibited from generally releasing information from its records. However, a DMV may confirm that a given license number and name match their records, and that there are no unresolved charges against that particular license. Someone attempting to confirm information you provide will receive "official verification" that you are who you say you are. Remember, you have just presented your Oregon driver's license in the name of John Doe, License # 12345-JD, and the Oregon DMV has confirmed that that information matches their records.

Now that you have some identification in the name of your victim, it's a simple matter to begin building on that identity. Rent a post office box in the victim's name. They will ask for two pieces of identification when you rent the box, but it's almost a formality. They record the ID types and numbers on the box application, you give the postal clerk a few dollars, and you have a mailbox for a year. As long as the ID presented is of reasonable quality, there should be no problem.

Next is a bank account. Here is where the crime of identity theft can become profitable. Once you have an account established, you can begin to obtain cash, credit, and merchandise in the victim's name.

To open an account in a bank you will need to produce the oft-demanded two pieces of ID, one of which must contain a photo. This is no big deal. You already have ID in your victim's name. It is also possible to open an account with many banks through the mail. You will still have to fill out applications and will probably be asked to include a photocopy of your driver's license with the application. However, through the mail, you have no face-to-face contact with anyone from the bank. This option may be the best if your fake ID is of not-so-good quality or if you just can't pull off this scam face-to-face.

On the other hand, going into the bank and opening an account has some major advantages. First, you are not filling out complete pen and paper applications. You will very likely sit down with a new accounts representative who will ask you to answer various questions — name, address, etc. — while he enters the information into a computer. You will have to produce a driver's license and some secondary piece of identification, but again this is no big deal. When I last opened a bank account, the new accounts representative asked for my driver's license number, which I simply read off while looking at something through the scuffed-up plastic window in a section of my wallet. I offered a department store credit card as secondary ID, which was accepted without question. The fact that I could answer the questions asked and show even the most basic form of identification was more than enough to open an account. As long as all the little blocks on the computer form got filled in, there was never any question. After all, I am putting money into the bank when I open an account. Customer service is the name of the game, and most people, bankers included, are not expecting people to be committing a fraud.

If you have sufficient information about a person to fill out a credit card application, you can likely obtain a credit card in the name of any person who has good enough credit to actually obtain the card himself. This is possible because most credit granters will run a credit check on persons applying for credit. The credit check will report that the individual identified on the application has a credit file, has an acceptable payment history and such, but there is no security protocol to ensure that the person who submitted the application is actually the person whose information is contained therein.

So, an identity thief using your personal information applies for and receives a credit card in your name. Now he can take this card and go on a shopping spree until the card reaches its maximum limit, then simply abandon it, leaving you to explain the charges and attempt to repair your damaged credit rating. A more adventurous identity thief might make a few purchases and actually pay the bill for a month or two. This would "validate" the card and allow him to continue to build on your stolen identity.

An identity thief can, over a short period of time, assume your entire identity. He can obtain an "official copy" of your birth certificate simply by writing to the birth records office in the place where you were born, and claim to be you, request a copy of your birth certificate, and enclose the three to eight dollars administrative fee.

He can contact the Department of Motor Vehicles where you had your license issued and request a replacement, claiming to have lost the original. This results in a temporary license being sent through the mail to the individual in question. If the identity thief is thinking about this, he writes to the DMV a month or so before, and provides a change of address to the DMV. Now when he requests a replacement license, the temporary license is sent to the new mailing address on record with the DMV. This temporary license can be used to obtain a new driver's license in another state.

Safeguarding Your Identity

It is important to be aware that if someone is using your identity, you may not even realize that anything is amiss until extensive damage has been done. This is why it is essential to safeguard your personal information and be aware of what information about you may be contained in the various records and databases maintained by government and business organizations.

Credit Reports
One way to protect yourself against identity theft is to watch for unusual activity on your credit reports. You should order a copy of your credit report from each of the three major credit-reporting agencies, Equifax, Experian, and

TransUnion, at least once a year. It may be an even better idea to order your credit reports every six months.

A copy of your credit report will cost you about nine dollars from each of the credit-reporting agencies. Depending on which state you live in, you may be authorized a free copy of your credit report once per year under state law. Of course, if you are denied credit or employment because of information contained in a credit report, you are authorized a free copy of that credit report.

The addresses for the three major credit-reporting agencies are:

Equifax
PO Box 740241
Atlanta, GA 30374-0241
Tel: 800-685-1111

Experian (formerly TRW)
PO Box 2002
Allen, TX 75013
Tel: 888-EXPERIAN (397-3742)

TransUnion
PO Box 1000
Chester, PA 19022
Tel: 800-916-8800

Once you have copies of your credit reports, it is important to review them carefully for accuracy and unexpected inquiries. Are all the accounts listed on your credit report accounts that you have opened? Are all listed open accounts ones that you are currently using? If there are accounts listed on your credit reports that you don't recognize, someone may have opened accounts in your name. If there are old accounts listed on your credit report that you are no longer using, be sure that these accounts are listed as closed. If there is activity on an account after you have stopped using it, you should definitely question this. If you are no longer using accounts that are listed on your credit report, contact the places where you established these accounts and close the accounts. Make sure that they are listed as closed by you when you get your next copies of your credit reports.

Along with checking accuracy of the accounts, confirm that all addresses on your credit reports are accurate. Incorrect addresses listed on your credit reports may indicate that someone is using your identity. Any inaccurate information on your credit reports should be disputed with the credit reporting agencies, and they should make adjustments to your credit reports so that they accurately reflect your credit history.

If you find errors on your credit report, it is cause for concern, but certainly not a reason to panic or believe that you must be the victim of identity theft. As many as two-thirds of all credit reports contain some type of factual error, and as many as one-third of all credit reports contain errors serious enough to result in denial of credit.

Finally, look at the list of inquiries at the bottom of your credit report. Whenever a company requests or receives a copy of your credit report, a notation is made on your report. Inquiries from companies that you do not deal with may indicate that someone is dealing with these companies using your name and personal information. Remember, you should have already opted-out of allowing the credit bureaus to sell your credit information for prescreened offers. Thus, any inquiries on your credit report should be only from those companies with which you are personally conducting business.

Other Records

In addition to obtaining copies of your credit reports, you may want to obtain copies of other records maintained about you, for instance, your driving record and Social Security Statement. Contact the Department of Motor Vehicles or Department of Licensing in your state. Be sure that your driving record is accurate and someone is not impersonating you.

Requests for your Social Security Statement should be on SSA Form 7004, but a letter providing your full name, Social Security number, and date and place of birth will also work. Do you have a passport? Find out if one has been issued in your name by sending a written request, including your full name and date and place of birth.

The Medical Information Bureau maintains records about the medical history of people, for employment and insurance purposes. Do they have a record about you? If they do, is it accurate, or is someone using your identity? Request a copy of your MIB record and find out.

If you served in the military, there will be information about you on file with the Defense Security Service. This is especially true if you held a security clearance or a position of trust and responsibility while in the service. You can obtain a copy of your background investigation.

The addresses for requesting this information are listed below.

Medical Information Bureau
MIB, Inc.
PO Box 105
Essex Station
Boston, MA 02112
Tel: 617-426-3660
Web site: www.mib.com

Defense Security Service
Privacy Act Branch
601 10th Street, Suite 128
Fort George G. Meade, MD 20755-5134

Social Security Administration
Wilkes Barre Data Operations Center
PO Box 7004
Wilkes Barre, PA 18767-7004

U.S. Department of State/Passport Office
Research & Liaison Branch
1111 19th Street NW, Suite 500
Washington, DC 20524

These records, and perhaps many others, may contain information about you. You should be aware of just what information is being maintained in various corporate and government databases. Furthermore, if that information contains errors, you should be able to correct those errors. Being aware of what information is being maintained about you, and by whom, makes it much easier to detect fraudulent use of that information or attempts to steal your identity.

Finally, for more information about identity theft, or for assistance if you believe that you are the victim of identity theft, you can contact the Federal Trade Commission at:

Identity Theft Clearinghouse
Federal Trade Commission
600 Pennsylvania Avenue, NW
Washington, DC 20580
Tel: 1-877-IDTHEFT (438-4338)
Web site: www.consumer.gov/idtheft

Chapter Five
Telemarketing

You are just sitting down to dinner when you receive a call from some telemarketer offering you the deal of a lifetime, or perhaps this is the one day during the week when you get to sleep in, but a ringing telephone steals those few extra hours of sleep from you. There are numerous legitimate telemarketers interrupting us at home and at work with various offers. While most people find these interruptions annoying at best, a significant number of people fall for the sales pitches of telemarketers and end up buying something that ten minutes before they weren't even thinking about.

Legitimate telemarketers stay in business because they realize that they can, through sales pitches, get a great number of people to purchase something they may not really want or need. Con men make use of the telemarketing approach because the same people who will purchase from a legitimate telemarketer can be scammed by a conman on the telephone. Unfortunately, it is very difficult to differentiate between the legitimate telemarketer hawking some product and the con man out to take you for every dollar you have.

Both the legitimate telemarketer and the con man will have some type of deal for you. Both will make their offer enticing, and both will have answers to any objections you may have.

The legitimate telemarketer may in fact have a worthwhile product, while the con man has nothing but a desire to obtain your hard-earned money. If either the telemarketer or con man can get you to agree to accept their deal, they will want some form of payment. This is usually a request for your credit card number, but may also be a request to send money to a given address. There will also be a request that you provide personal information, which will at least include your full name and address.

The problem is that you can't tell from the telephone call whether the offer is legitimate or not. It is a very bad idea to disclose your personal and financial information over the telephone to anyone, unless you initiated the call.

Dealing With Telemarketers

If you receive a call from anyone attempting to sell something, you should respond by asking them to answer the following questions before letting them proceed with any offer they may have.

1. Is this a telemarketing call?

2. What is your full name?

3. What company do you represent?

4. What is the address and telephone number of the company you represent?

By law, a telemarketer must identify that the call is a sales call and state who they represent before they give their sales pitch. However, if they actually do this, it tends to be tossed in with a bunch of other babble at the beginning of the call when you are not ready to copy that information. "Hello, my name is John with Run Amok Industries. How are you today?" The telemarketer or con man is now expecting an answer to his question, "How are you today?" thus establishing a conversation with you and letting him launch into his sales pitch.

You must not engage this individual in conversation before having clear answers to the above questions. If the caller tries to put off your questions or delays answering them, it's a scam. The law requires that telemarketers provide this information to those from whom they solicit business. Any telemarketer who will not provide the information when you ask, is acting illegally and you should certainly not deal with this criminal. A legitimate telemarketer wants to give his sales pitch, but will also be willing to clearly answer these basic questions up front. A con man may also be able to answer these questions, but may be a little hesitant to do so right at the beginning of the call, as it breaks the flow and patter of the scam.

Write down the answers to the above questions along with the date and time of the call. Then you can choose to listen to the rest of the sales pitch or end the call. However, it is safest to never buy anything from a telemarketing call and you should probably end the call in this way:

1. "I never buy anything from telemarketers."

2. "Please add me to your 'Do Not Call' list and don't call me again."

3. Hang up.

You may want to employ these three simple steps after receiving a "yes" answer to "Is this a telemarketing call?" However, fully identifying the telemarketer before ending the call allows you to identify calls from them in the future as criminal activity.

Federal law, specifically the Telephone Consumer Protection Act of 1991, requires that once you instruct a telemarketer not to call you, they must add you to their "Do Not Call" list and not make further contact with you. Furthermore, the law provides for a private right of action against telemarketers who recontact you once you have instructed them not to do so. This private right of action is one good reason to fully identify a telemarketer before telling them to get lost. You should also consider that no legitimate telemarketer will recontact you after you have told them not to: a repeat call is almost certainly a scam.

Inmate Employees

There is another danger that comes from disclosing information to a telemarketer. Some legitimate telemarketers use inmates as part of their telemarketing labor force. Yes, you read that correctly. The person calling you with a telemarketing offer may in fact be an inmate at some prison. Do you really want to disclose your personal and financial information to someone whom society has deemed such a threat that he must be incarcerated?

In February 2000, the teenage daughter of Texas resident April Jordan answered a telemarketing call from Utah's SandStar Family Entertainment, a company that makes family-oriented films. The telemarketing call was placed by an inmate in a Utah prison working as a telemarketer as part of the Utah prison's work program. During this call, the inmate obtained personal information from Ms. Jordan's teenage daughter. This young girl later received a sexually suggestive letter from another prison inmate in Utah as a result of the information she had disclosed during the telemarketing call.

A sexually suggestive letter sent to a young girl from a prison inmate is certainly a serious problem. It can cause the girl to feel unsafe in her own home, as well as suffer other forms of mental anguish, but it could have been worse. What would have happened if our inmate telemarketer had passed the information he learned to a criminal associate outside of prison? What if he had given the information to a sexual predator near this young girl's hometown?

A large number of states allow prisoners to work as telemarketers. Many companies use prison labor because they are able to obtain it at a lower wage than might be required to hire honest men and women seeking employment. However, when you receive a telemarketing call from an inmate, you have no way of knowing that you are speaking with and disclosing personal information to someone who is in prison. There is no requirement that they identify themselves as inmates.

Do Not Call Lists

First, of course, is to have a policy of never dealing with telemarketers. You really have no idea who is calling you during a telemarketing call. It could be a con man trying to gather your personal information as part of a scam or identity theft. Even if the call is made on behalf of a legitimate business, you could be disclosing your personal information to a prison inmate who can't be trusted to use it only for the purpose for which you provided it.

Next, register with the Direct Marketing Association's Telephone Preference Service (page 71). Most legitimate direct marketers —telemarketers — are members of the Direct Marketing Association (DMA). The DMA maintains a list of people who have registered their telephone numbers as those who do not want to receive telemarketing calls. By adding your telephone number to the list, you will limit the number of telemarketing calls you receive. Simply send a letter to the DMA, include your telephone number, and ask that you be placed on their "Do Not Call" List.

While most legitimate telemarketers are members of the DMA and honor requests that they not call numbers listed on the Telephone Preference Service's "Do Not Call" List, there are still many telemarketers who are not members of the DMA.

We have already seen that the Telephone Consumer Protection Act of 1991 makes it illegal for telemarketers to call you once you have told them not to do so. And we have discussed how to handle calls when you answer the telephone only to find out that you are being interrupted by a telemarketer. However, what about calls made when you are not home? Well, obviously, if you are not at home, the call won't affect you, but if the call is from a telemarketer, your number will still be on their list of numbers to call. They will continue to call until they get an answer.

One way to deal with this problem is to include a message on your answering machine that instructs telemarketers to add you to their "Do Not Call" list and not to call you again. The Telephone Consumer Protection Act of 1991 says, that once you notify a telemarketer not to call you, they may not legally do so again. Putting this type of notice on your answering machine will get you added to the "Do Not Call" lists of legitimate telemarketers that attempt to contact you when you are not home.

Try the following message on your answering machine.

Hello. If you are a telemarketer, add this number to your "Do Not Call" list, and do not call here again. We will not conduct any type of business with telemarketers, or as part of a telephone solicitation. Everyone else, please leave a message at the tone.

This will give notice to legitimate telemarketers that you will not conduct business with them, and they will add your number to their "Do Not Call" list. Legitimate telemarketers want to talk with people who might be interested in what they are selling or who can be talked into buying. Once you have made it clear that you will never deal with a telephone solicitor of any type, they will not waste their time calling you again, unless they are running some type of criminal scam.

Predictive Dialers

There is one other type of calling used by telemarketers that, while not illegal, is certainly annoying. How would you feel about a business that called your home every day, let your telephone ring two or three times and then hung up before you could answer it? Many telemarketers do just that through the use of predictive dialers. A predictive dialer is a device that simultaneously calls multiple numbers — causing them all to ring — and then routes the first call answered to a telemarketer and dumps the remainder of the calls. Thus, your telephone may ring two or three times, but there will be no one there when you answer, if someone else in the multiple numbers dialed has answered first and the predictive dialer has dumped the remainder of the calls.

The idea of predictive dialers is that they do the labor-intensive dialing of numbers, screening out busy and nonfunctioning numbers, thereby keeping the telemarketers connected to people so they can make their sales pitch. If you get a number of hang-up calls, it may very well be a telemarketer using predictive dialers to call numbers in your area. Because predictive dialers attempt to screen out nonfunctioning numbers, it is possible to cause some predictive dialers to log your telephone number as nonfunctioning by adding a special information tone to the beginning of your answering machine message and having your machine answer incoming calls on the first ring.

The special information tone is that short series of tones you hear when you call a nonfunctioning number or a number that has been changed. Simply find a nonfunctioning telephone number and record the special information tone, which is played before the telephone company's message. Add this special information tone as the first thing one hears on your answering machine message. Predictive dialers that receive this tone when calling you will log your telephone number as nonfunctioning. Humans calling you will simply listen to whatever voice message you have recorded immediately following the special information tone.

With all the obvious problems associated with telemarketing, are there any legitimate businesses using telemarketing to promote their products and services? If you accept an offer presented by a telemarketer is there any chance that you will actually get what you paid for? Yes, there are certainly legitimate businesses conducting telemarketing and if you deal with a legitimate business as part of a telemarketing offer, you will likely receive whatever it is that you have agreed to purchase.

However, the potential for fraud is so high when dealing with a telemarketing call that any benefit you may receive from a legitimate offer is massively outweighed by the risk of fraud. Even if you happen to receive a legitimate offer, what do you know about the character of the individual to whom you are giving your personal information, credit card number or bank account number? We have seen that legitimate telemarketers use incarcerated felons to conduct their telemarketing calls, and the danger of disclosing your personal information to a known criminal should be obvious.

When it comes to dealing with a telemarketer, just say no.

Slamming and Cramming

What are slamming and cramming? It sounds like the latest music to which our teenagers are listening. In this case, however, it has to do with a scam perpetrated by various telephone service providers.

Slamming

Slamming is changing your telephone service provider without your authorization. If you think your telephone service is being provided by AT&T, but find that it has been changed to MCI, Sprint, or Joe Scam's Telephone Company, you are a victim of slamming.

Slamming can occur in a variety of different ways. A telemarketing call may get you to inadvertently agree to "try a new telephone service" during the call. Filling out sweepstakes entries received in the constant flood of junk mail in our mailboxes may entail a new telephone service provider as part of the sweepstakes entry. Failure to return a postage-paid card included with some offer in which you have participated may also be used as a way to claim you have consented to switching your telephone service provider. There may be fees involved in switching telephone service providers. Your new — and unauthorized — service provider may charge higher rates, resulting in a higher monthly phone bill for you.

You may only notice that your telephone service provider has changed if you notice a new name in the long-distance portion of your telephone bill. Too often, however, when we receive our telephone bills, we look at the amount due and maybe scan the list of numbers billed to us that month. Then, we just mutter something about the high cost of telephone service and send in the payment.

To protect yourself from slamming, it is important to pay attention to all the information recorded on your telephone bill. One can also call the telephone service number at 1-700-555-4141 and a recording will tell you which long-distance provider is associated with the number from which you placed the call. This call is toll-free. It may be useful to use this number to confirm your long-distance service provider any time you are presented with a telemarketing offer to change your telephone service.

Another very effective method of protecting yourself from slamming is to have Primary Interexchange Carrier protection added to your telephone lines. This is a free service and is simply an order on file with your local telephone company requiring that they receive and confirm specific authorization from you before making any change to your long-distance service.

Cramming

Cramming is adding various services to your telephone service without your authorization. These services may include such things as voice mail, selective call forwarding, priority calling, selective call rejection, and more. If you fail to read your telephone bills carefully, you may end up paying for services you never actually requested. Many people don't catch on to this scam until they have overpaid their bills for months at a time.

To prevent cramming, it is important to take time to carefully read all the information on your telephone bills. Know what you are being charged for and make sure that you have authorized each and every one of the charges on your telephone bill. Cramming is an effective scam, because two or three dollars billed to thousands of customers adds up over time, yet will often go unnoticed, or at least unchallenged, by the majority of telephone customers. Be sure that you know exactly what service was provided for each of those little service charges you see on your telephone bill. If you see a charge that is unfamiliar or that you don't understand, call your telephone company's billing office and get an explanation of that charge.

Finally, if you feel you are the victim of slamming or cramming and cannot get the matter quickly resolved by dealing with your local telephone company, you should call the Federal Communications Commission at 1-888-225-5322 for further assistance.

Chapter Six
Street Cons

When a stranger approaches you, on the street — beware. Almost all such offers of special deals or great opportunities will be scams. Legitimate companies simply don't do business this way.

There are, of course, street cons which everyone knows are scams, such as "Three Card Monte" or the "Shell Game," where one tries to find a specific card or the pea under the shell as the con man moves them about. These games can't be won. Unfortunately, there are still people who will play these games on the street, thinking they can win a little money from this guy running a game on the street corner. However, most street cons are not as obvious as "Three Card Monte" and the "Shell Game."

Lotto Scam

In this scam, the victim is approached by a con man, who says that he has a winning lotto ticket, but that he is unable to claim his winnings because he is in the country illegally.

The con man usually doesn't claim to have won the multi-million dollar jackpot, but a more believable winning of several thousand dollars. The con man offers to split the winnings with you if you will help him claim his prize. With almost any Lotto ticket where the winning value is more than a couple hundred dollars, you cannot simply take the ticket into a store, but will have to cash it in at the state Lotto commission/gaming board or similar agency. There will be ID requirements, taxes, etc. — all of which will pose a problem for someone in the country illegally. About this time, someone — the con man's partner — will approach and suggest that perhaps our con man should not just give his lottery ticket to you to cash in and expect you to then split the winnings. He will suggest that before you can go cash the ticket you should post a little "good faith money." Maybe not half of the expected winnings, but at least enough to demonstrate good faith on your part. The idea behind the "good faith money" is that, once you have the winning Lotto ticket in hand, you may very well decide not to share the money.

He will suggest that you all go to your bank and withdraw your good faith money, and then go cash in the lottery ticket as a group. The con men have certainly shown you a lottery ticket, and probably a newspaper clipping listing winning numbers that match the ticket's numbers. They keep up their patter, their excitement at the upcoming winnings, and they convince you that you too will soon share these winnings. Of course, the validity of a lottery ticket can be confirmed at any place that sells lottery tickets, but our con men make sure that you don't have the chance to make this simple check.

Should you become hesitant to complete this deal or want to make too many checks, the third party to the scam will suggest that maybe they don't need you anyway, that he will post the money, cash the ticket, and split the winnings with the "illegal alien". It now looks like you will be cut out of the deal and lose your share of the winning ticket. The potential of a share of the winnings, the excitement generated by the con men, and now the possibility of being cut out of the deal often has the victim of this scam hurrying to come up with the "good faith money" before it's too late. Of course, once you have withdrawn money from the bank and given it to one of these con men as your "good faith money" in this deal, they only need to make their getaway and leave you holding a worthless lottery ticket.

The Lotto Scam, like others of its kind, could be easily prevented by a reasonable degree of caution. Ask why the initial holder of the ticket — the illegal alien — would approach you. Doesn't he have friends or associates who are legally in the country with whom he could split his winnings in exchange for helping him cash in the ticket? Before investing your "good faith money" shouldn't you confirm the validity of the winning ticket?

Lost and Found

In this scam, a well-dressed woman approaches the intended victim of the scam, claiming to have lost a valuable ring or other piece of jewelry. This scam is targeted at someone in charge of an area open to the public, such as a store, used car lot, or perhaps a park or recreational area. A potential victim is simply someone, such as an employee or manager, that you might report a lost item to.

The woman describes the lost jewelry and requests assistance in searching for it. Of course, it isn't found. She explains that she is sure she lost it around here and, while it has some intrinsic value, it has a great deal of sentimental value to her. She offers a reward of $1,000 if you find it, and leaves her name and telephone number.

Later in the day, someone will apparently find the missing piece of jewelry, and will mention it to the person to whom the woman has offered the reward for its return.

The person "finding" the jewelry will say that he intends to pawn it for two hundred or maybe even three hundred dollars. The victim of this scam sees his $1,000 reward quickly slipping away if the person who just found the "lost" jewelry takes it to the nearest pawnshop. Of course, telling the person who found the ring that the owner of the ring has offered a reward for its return and left her telephone number simply means that the reward goes to someone else. If he simply tells the "finder" that he knows who the jewelry belongs to and asks for it, the "finder" claims disbelief but allows that something might be able to be worked out.

The finder of the jewelry is, of course, in cahoots with the woman who "lost" it earlier that day. Instead of having to go through the trouble of pawning the jewelry, he will let the victim "convince" him to sell the jewelry right there for the $200 he was planning to get from a pawnshop. The victim gives up $200 in exchange for the "lost" piece of jewelry, thinking he can now call the woman who lost it, claim the $1,000 reward, and come out $800 ahead.

Needless to say, the telephone number left by the woman who lost the jewelry doesn't work, and if the victim tries to sell the jewelry himself to recover his loss, he finds that it is cheap costume jewelry worth no more than forty or fifty dollars.

This scam can be run at several places at the same time, with the con artists making $200-$300 minus the cost of the costume jewelry each time it is successful. If the potential victim of the scam can't be maneuvered into offering a couple hundred dollars for the jewelry, the "finder" simply leaves with it to try the scam somewhere else.

Coin Con

This scam is similar to the Lost and Found scam. In this case, you are approached on the street by a person who appears to be mentally retarded. He has a collection of coins that he apparently found and points out a label on the album: *John Smith, Capital Numismatic Society — Tel: 555-7283.* The "retarded" person in possession of this coin collection gets you to call the number on the album. The call is answered by another player in this scam who offers you a reward of $500 for return of the coins. He gives you directions to his home to return the coins, and asks if you would be so kind as to give the poor guy who found them $100. If you will do so, he will give you your $100 back as well as the $500 reward. He gets you to pass the telephone to the "retarded" person in possession of the coins so that he can thank him for finding them, too. He also apparently tells him that you will give him $100 for the coins.

The retarded person is now expecting you to give him $100 in exchange for the coins and won't give them up without his "reward." You have the name, address, and telephone number of the owner of these coins, and a promise of a $500 reward as well as your $100 back which you are supposed to give to the retarded person.

You give the guy his $100 and take the coin collection to the address you were given, only to find yourself standing in an empty lot, holding a bunch of cheap foreign coins worth, maybe, ten bucks. If you are able to track down the telephone number listed on the album, you will find that it turns out to be a pay phone somewhere, and that the person playing Mr. Smith is long gone.

Jamaican Switch and Other Sleight-of-Hand Scams

In this scam, the victim is approached by a person claiming to be from Jamaica or some other country, who requests some type of assistance. He offers to pay for this assistance and shows that he is in possession of a large amount of cash.

About this time, a third person approaches and cautions the "Jamaican" about the dangers of carrying around large amounts of cash. He says that the money should be deposited in a bank. The Jamaican says that he doesn't trust banks, explaining that it is often difficult to withdraw money once it is deposited. He says, however, that if the victim can show that it is easy to make a withdrawal, he will open an account and put money in the bank.

The victim and the Jamaican go to the bank where the victim makes a withdrawal to demonstrate the ease of doing so.

Taking the money the victim has just withdrawn from the bank, perhaps via an ATM, the Jamaican explains that in Jamaica one way to carry money safely on the street is to carry it tied in a handkerchief in an inside coat pocket. Wrapping the victim's money in a handkerchief, he gives it to the victim, who places it in his coat, as the Jamaican has described.

The Jamaican and the victim now part ways. However, when the victim removes the handkerchief from his coat and unwraps his money, he finds only cut up newspaper. The handkerchief with the money has been switched for one containing worthless pieces of newspaper. Simple sleight-of-hand, but the victim has still lost his money.

The Jamaican Switch was originally done in the manner just described, but can also be done where money is placed in an envelope, cash bag, or other item which conceals it from view and can be switched for a duplicate item containing cut-up newspaper.

Street Corner Shopping

Like the Jamaican Switch, here we have another scam involving sleight-of-hand. "Hey, buddy, are you interested in buying a new video camera at a great price?" You are approached on the street and offered the chance to buy some item at a great price. These cameras sell for more than $1,000 if you buy them from a store, but the street vendor has a couple that he can sell at a great discount, just $300.

"Take a look. It's a working video camera. Here's the box and all of the accessories. I've only got a couple left, but if you want one, it's yours. I'll pack it up for you. I'll put it right here in the box with the accessories you just looked at. Let me put the box in this bag so you can carry it. Okay, that's $300 please. Thanks, been a pleasure doing business with you. Let your friends know."

So, did you just buy a camera stolen from a warehouse somewhere? There has certainly been a theft; you will find out about it when you get home and open the box containing your new camera, only to find that it contains some rocks or maybe a brick. The seller of the bargain-priced video camera packed it up in front of you, placed it in a bag so you could carry it easily, and while you were momentarily distracted, he or his partner in this crime made a switch for the box of rocks. Switching packages is not particularly difficult, especially on a busy street corner or in a crowded marketplace.

Once the victim of this crime discovers that he has been left holding a bag of rocks, it is too late. The criminal is long gone, and the victim will probably be hesitant to go to the police. Explaining to the police how you were trying to buy a $1,000 camera for $300 from somebody on the street, meaning it was probably stolen to begin with, doesn't make for a great ending to a bad day.

Likewise, if you are buying what the seller claims to be an original product of high quality, beware. The deal that is too good to be true is almost always a scam. I have seen Chanel No. 19 perfume sold on the street for $25 per half-ounce and Rolex watches sold for $500. This same perfume sold in a reputable store for $69 per quarter-ounce and the Rolex watch sold for $3,000 at a reputable jeweler. Needless to say, the products sold on the street were fakes, but the people selling them insisted that they were genuine. Unfortunately, there were others looking at these same items that seemed to believe the seller's claims that they were genuine.

If you are going to buy some item from a vendor on a street corner or from some guy running a business out of the trunk of his car, pay extra attention to what you are getting. Watch your purchases with extra care and ask yourself if you are really getting the deal you think you are. Remember, if the product breaks the day after you get it home, you will probably not get a refund from whomever sold it to you. You probably won't even be able to find him again.

Panhandlers

Panhandlers are a part of almost every city and even many rural areas. While panhandling may be the only means of survival for a few, many panhandlers are not homeless and may not be destitute. Furthermore, many communities researching this matter have determined that, rather than supporting the poor, panhandling feeds drug addiction and alcoholism and perpetuates homelessness. (Alice S. Baum and Donald W. Burns, *A Nation in Denial: The Truth About Homelessness,* Boulder, CO: Westview Press, 1993.)

It is important to understand that panhandling — approaching people on a public street and asking them for money — is not a crime in and of itself. The U.S. Supreme Court has held that panhandling is protected as a form of free speech under the 1st Amendment to the Constitution. Aggressive panhandling may violate other laws if panhandlers are blocking traffic or access to public buildings, or if their demands for a hand-out become threatening. However, laws specifically prohibiting the act of panhandling itself have been ruled unconstitutional.

While we may want to help the poor and those suffering some misfortune, giving money to panhandlers is not the way to go about it. If approached by a panhandler, a firm but polite "No" or "Sorry, not today" will usually resolve the matter. Don't just ignore a person who asks you for money, any more than you would ignore someone who asked you the time, and there is certainly no call to be rude or insulting toward this person. Just because a person is spending much of his time on the streets, is dirty, or is addicted to drugs and alcohol, does not mean he is less than human. However, giving a buck or two to a panhandler is not going to do anything to resolve the problem of homelessness or poverty in the area. Certainly, give what you can to help those in need, but give your money and volunteer some time to organizations in your area that can actually do some good for these people and make changes for the better in the community.

Chapter Seven
Other Scams and Frauds

There are numerous other areas that are subject to scams and frauds, including investments, charities, repair, and even police interaction. These areas will be covered in this chapter, but first, it is important to discuss a group that seems particularly vulnerable to scams and has been increasingly targeted by con men. Consequently, this group also is the subject of more attention from law enforcement officials.

Targeting the Elderly

While anyone can be the target of a hoax, scam, or fraud, these crimes often target the elderly. What makes the elderly such attractive targets?

One of the reasons that criminals target the elderly is that the elderly may have more assets to steal. A person who has worked thirty or forty years probably has something in savings. His mortgage may be paid off, or at least have built up considerable equity. He may have other items of value acquired over the years, making him a valuable target for a con man out to see what he can steal.

On the other hand, it may be that the elderly person being targeted by criminals doesn't have a lot of assets, perhaps only a couple thousand dollars in savings. In this case, the criminal will try to make his elderly victim believe that there will be a large and rapid return on the investment of those dollars. The idea here is to make the victim believe that he can make up for a lifetime of no investments or savings by entrusting the con man with whatever money the victim may be able to come up with.

Elderly people may live alone, their spouse passed on and their children grown. With families moving at ever-increasing distances from each other — other towns, different states, perhaps on the far side of the country —there is often no close family nearby. The person living alone may be lonely, and this is an emotion on which the criminal can play. Additionally, fifty or sixty years ago, the pace of life was different and people tended to be more "neighborly" and trusting strangers. Many elderly people may find it difficult to see the con man as a criminal. The elderly victim of a scam may simply be too polite to tell the con man "No" with sufficient force and finality that he realizes his scam won't work on this person.

Finally, some people, as they grow older, may suffer from decreased mental capacity and failing memory. This is by no means a guaranteed effect of aging, but is sufficiently common to be worth considering. There is even the joke which refers to someone who forgets something or loses his train of thought as having a "senior moment."

Targeting Indications

There are some fairly good indicators that an elderly person — or anyone else for that matter — may have been targeted as part of a scam.

- The person receives a large number of calls asking for charitable donations, claiming that the person has won some kind of prize or award, or offering investment and money-making opportunities.

- The person ends up with a number of cheap prizes, for example, pen and pencil sets, costume jewelry, or a small appliance. These items may have been purchased in an effort to win larger prizes that will never be awarded.

- The person suddenly makes a number of unusual withdrawals from his accounts, or tries to acquire sums of money that are out of the ordinary for his normal activities.

- The person suddenly becomes secretive about his financial affairs. This is more than maintaining a degree of privacy about those affairs, but reflects a sudden change with family or close friends regarding the discussion of financial matters.

- The person suddenly begins having financial problems or difficulty paying bills. This indicates a reallocation of funds that had previously been used to pay expenses.

If you find that you have become a victim of some kind of hoax, scam, or fraud, it is very important that you report this crime immediately. If you become aware of an elderly friend or family member — or any friend or family member for that matter — that may be the victim of some kind of a hoax, scam, or fraud, it is likewise very important that this information be reported to the proper authorities.

Too often, after finding that they have been scammed, people are embarrassed. They feel foolish and may want to hide the fact that they were so easily taken in by a con man. Thus, the crime goes unreported and leaves the criminal free to perpetrate his crimes again against his next victim.

When we sit and read a book about hoaxes, scams, and frauds, it is easy to say "only a total fool would fall for that." However, people who are in no way foolish or stupid become victims of these crimes everyday. The criminal committing these hoaxes, scams, and acts of fraud is simply taking advantage of a weakness he has found in the way someone maintains the security of his personal affairs. The only foolish or stupid victim of this type of a crime is the person who does not report it or does not take steps to prevent it once he is aware of the potential risks.

Investment Fraud

Investment fraud and scams associated with investments can be difficult to prove. The difference between a scam and simply a bad investment is a matter of intent. Does the individual(s) offering the investment intend to scam you out of your money or did the planned outcome of the investment just never come to pass?

While I was writing this book, some friends whom I have known for many years began looking at making some new investments and making some adjustments in their finances. While making these new financial plans, they met with some "investment advisors" who came to their home and offered a complete financial plan to get them out of debt and leave them with more than one million dollars at the maturity of this new investment.

After the meeting, my friends were excited about the possibility of their new investment and the amount of money they would make, how they would be able to consolidate their debts into "one low monthly payment," and quickly become debt free. Listening to the claims these "investment advisors" had made, I began to wonder why everyone was not following this amazing new investment scheme. With the old saying, "If it sounds too good to be true, it probably is," firmly in mind, I too met with the investment advisors to see just what their investment plan — or scam — was.

During the meeting, the investment advisors were certainly excited about their plan. They even had a book full of pictures of smiling people who had made a million dollars with their investment plan. They told me how I could save several hundred thousand dollars by remortgaging my home with them. My investments of several years were okay, they guessed, but by turning these investments over to them to manage, I would be much more successful. And, of course, I needed a better insurance plan. Their plan only cost a few dollars more per month, but it really was a much better plan. I wouldn't have to worry about all the details: if I would just sign a few forms, they would take care of everything. Don't mind the blanks on the forms, "that's just administrative data we need to fill in back at the office." All I had to do was trust them, sit back, and grow rich. Trust and friendship were words they used frequently during our discussion. Remember, though, that I had only met these people an hour ago.

As you read this, does the whole investment plan sound like something a farmer should be shoveling to fertilize his fields? It's pretty clear when you read about it in a book about hoaxes, frauds, and scams. During the couple of hours I sat and talked with these people, their fraud wasn't so clear. They had answers to any objection I raised. After all, they were my "friends." I could trust them. They were excited about their plan and just wanted to share it with their new friend — me.

I told them I was also excited about the plan, but I really needed to think about it for a day or so. They didn't like the idea that I would not immediately sign up for their plan, but they would be glad to come back in a day or two so we could complete the paperwork.

After my new "friends," the investment advisors, left, I decided I would do a little checking into their background. First, I called the state office of the Department of Professional Licensing in my state and asked to speak to someone in the Securities Dealers and Investment Advisors Division. I wanted to know if there were any complaints filed against the individuals who wanted to handle my financial affairs and how long they had been licensed. Licensed? These people had no license to do what they were doing. In fact, the Department of Professional Licensing had no record of them whatsoever. What about the company they claimed to work for? Yes, the company existed, but a little checking revealed a current investigation by the Securities and Exchange Commission against the company, and a little further research found a couple of pending fraud cases in other states with this company listed as a defendant.

The next day I called the company and asked to speak with my new investment advisors. They weren't in at the moment but they would be sure to call me back before lunch. Did I want to leave any message? I said I had spoken with the Department of Professional Licensing and there didn't seem to be any record of their license, and there seemed to be some kind of a problem between their company and the SEC. I would like to clear up these concerns before I committed to any investment with them.

Needless to say, they never returned my call. I even tried to get in touch with them a couple more times, but they were never in; they still have never returned my calls. Scam artists hate informed inquiry more than vampires hate the noonday sun.

There are plenty of other people who will believe the scam, sign over investments and remortgage their homes, and will come up with just that little bit of extra money to invest into their plan. I guess these investment advisors don't want to be my new friends after all.

Charity Fraud

Most men of good character are willing to help out someone in need. We have all probably dropped change in a jar at the check-out line in some store or given a couple of dollars to kids going door-to-door during the holiday season collecting money to "help the less fortunate." We may have written a check to contribute to some cause we thought worthy. But just how much of the money we contributed actually went to the cause we thought we were supporting and how much of our contribution was used to pay administrative fees, salaries, and expenses of the organization promoting the charity?

Simply put, it takes money to make money. An organization soliciting donations for its cause will have to spend some amount of money to get the word out to the general public. If an organization is going to mail you a request for a donation, there is the obvious cost involved of printing the requests for donations and the cost of postage to mail them to likely contributors. Obviously, there are many other additional costs involved in fund raising. However, some charities spend more on administrative costs than actually goes to the cause the charity claims to be supporting.

The National Charities Information Bureau says that at least fifty percent of the money one donates to a charity should go to the stated purpose of the charity as opposed to fund raising and administrative expenses. Personally, I believe that at least seventy-five percent of the money donated to a charity should be directly used for the stated purpose of that charity.

Checking on Large Charities

Before donating to any charity, investigate that charity with one or all of the following organizations, and get information from that charity sent to you through the mail. Then if you feel moved to donate, you will be making an informed decision.

American Institute of Philanthropy
4905 Del Ray Avenue, Suite 300A
Bethesda, MD 20814
Tel: 301-913-5200
www.charitywatch.org

Council of Better Business Bureaus, Inc.
4200 Wilson Blvd.
Arlington, VA 22203
Tel: 703-276-0100
www.bbb.org

National Charities Information Bureau
19 Union Square West
New York, NY 10003
Tel: 212-929-6300
www.give.org

Before donating to any charity, it is generally a good idea to know exactly what it does with the money it receives. Anyone stopping to think about it for a few seconds will realize that people who work full-time for a charity must receive some type of compensation. But how much of your contributions to a charity should be allocated for compensation of its employees? Below is a list of some of the best-known charities and the reported compensation for their chief executive officers. Should the CEO of a charity be compensated for his or her efforts? Of course. Should that compensation be half a million dollars per year? How about a quarter million dollars or one hundred thousand dollars? Perhaps the CEO is worth a million dollars, but before you donate money, you should at least be aware of how it's being allocated.

Organization	Chief Executive Officer	CEO Compensation*
American Diabetes	John H. Graham IV	$320,949 (1998)
American Heart Association	M. Cass Wheeler	$414,114 (1999)
ASPCA	Larry Hawk, D.V.M.	$289.880 (2000)
Christian Children's Fund	John F. Schultz, Ph.D.	$185,172 (2000)

Doctors Without Borders	Joelle Tanguy	$91,322 (2000)
Humane Society of the U.S.	Paul G. Irwin	$288,848 (2000)
Make-A-Wish Foundation	Paula J. Van Ness	$100,906 (1998)
March of Dimes	Dr. Jennifer L. Howse	$414,481 (2000)
Muscular Dystrophy Assoc.	Robert Ross	$357,126 (1999)
NAACP	Kweisi Mfume	$220,723 (1999)
Salvation Army	John Busby	$87,470 (1999)
United Way of America	Betty Stanley Beene	$360,149 (2000)

* CEO Annual Compensation includes annual salary, benefit plans, expense accounts, and other compensation as applicable.

Before donating to any charity you should be able to answer the following questions:

- What is the exact purpose of the charity?

- What is the address and telephone number for the charity?

- Is your contribution tax deductible?

- What percentage of your donation goes to the charity's stated purpose as opposed to administrative fees, salaries, and operating costs?

If you can answer these four simple questions and feel moved to donate to the charity in question, by all means do so. If you cannot answer these questions, do not donate your money. The charity may be legitimate, but you don't know enough about it yet to be sure. On the other hand, the whole thing may be a scam, playing on your emotions and good will.

The Charity Jar Scam

Large established charities can be easily investigated and a determination made in a short time as to whether they are using donations in such a manner that you want to donate to them. However, local causes, police and fireman funds, and people collecting for churches and small charitable causes can be much more difficult to investigate. The jar at the checkout counter of your favorite store or restaurant, where you dropped a couple of dollars to support the local "firemen's fund" or contribute to the medical expenses of a "injured child," may very well be a scam. Many store and restaurant managers will allow someone to place a jar for contributions in their establishment without confirming that it is for a legitimate cause.

This charity-jar scam can be quite profitable. Consider a very small-scale scam using this setup. In order to run this scam, you put together twenty-five charity jars, neatly assembled and professional looking. You then find a cause that is drawing some public sympathy or support — firemen's fund, injured/ill children, victims of some disaster, etc. — and add the little "Please Help Support _____" sign to the jars. A skilled con man will have little difficulty getting twenty-five local establishments to put these jars at the check-out stands of their businesses. You stop by every week or two and collect the donations left in the jars. If each jar averages just ten dollars per day, at the end of the month you will have collected $7,500.

Let's say you decide to run this scam on a larger scale and put out one hundred of your scam charity jars. You spread them out over a few communities and run the scam for just one month. Maybe you are only able to average five dollars per jar every day. At the end of the month you have still made $15,000.

How much money did you make last month working a conventional job? There are certainly a number of legitimate charities and worthy causes that do in fact put out jars for you to donate your loose change or maybe a buck or two. That's why these scam charity jars work — you can't tell the difference between the real charities and worthy causes and the scams.

Imagine that you want to be really slick about this little scam and cover the possibility of any questions in the future. You take the money collected from your one hundred jars during the month and take $3421.50 to the local bank, where you get a certified check that you send off to the firemen's fund or whatever you claimed you were collecting for. You now pocket $11,578.50 in tax-free income.

The chances of ever getting caught running this scam are fairly slim. It usually runs for a short time: one month, maybe two. There are a bunch of collection jars scattered throughout the community, but only you really know how many. Nobody knows how much money is actually collected in the jars except you, because you tally up the money from each jar. Finally, if you ever get caught or there is ever a question about the donations, you have a copy of the check you sent from "all the money I collected" to help this worthy cause.

The next time you put a dollar in that collection jar, ask yourself if you are really sure who or what you are supporting.

Repair Fraud

Things break and require repair. There may be a problem with your automobile, the roof of your house may start to leak, or maybe your television just quit. Whatever the problem, unless you have the skill to make your own repairs, you will have to hire someone to make these repairs for you. Very few people have the skills to repair everything they own, from automobiles, to computers, to appliances, to the leaky roof of their home. Before having any major repairs made, it pays to get three or four estimates for the repair work. Even discounting the possibility of some type of fraud, it is a good idea to obtain repair estimates simply to get the best deal on the repairs you are having done.

Once you have decided that you will have repairs made by a specific contractor or repairman, you should get a written contract for those repairs. This contract should include the cost of repair parts, labor costs, the quality and type of materials to be used, and the starting and completion dates. Additionally, for major repairs such as home repair or home improvement projects, you should also require that the contractor provide you with a "Waiver of Lien," which states that he has paid for all material and labor as related to your contract. You will also want to ensure that the contractor has a Certificate of Liability Insurance, proving that he has insurance to cover any damage or injuries that may occur during the time he is working for you.

Certain contractors, such as electricians, plumbers, and builders working on structural items, are required to be licensed. Contact your state board of professional licensing to determine if the type of work you are planning to have done requires a license. If it does, be sure that the contractor you hire is properly licensed and insured. Also, be sure that the contractor obtains all necessary building permits before commencing any work. This may sound like a lot of information to require from a contractor, but it is for your own protection and legitimate contractors have this information readily available, providing it to clients as a matter of course.

Once you have chosen a contractor and are presented with a contract — most contractors have a standardized contract they use in their business — read the terms of the contract carefully. Don't be pressured into signing a contract without reading it, and don't sign it if it contains something you don't understand.

If you have small repairs made to your automobile or some appliance, always require that, if parts are replaced, the old parts are returned to you. One type of repair fraud consists of padding invoices by billing for replaced parts that were never actually replaced. By requiring the return of replaced parts, you can limit this type of fraud.

One of the best ways to protect yourself against repair fraud is to find a repairman before you need one. When your car won't start or the furnace doesn't run on a cold winter's night, you may find yourself accepting the first repairman that you can get to do the work. However, if you take the time now, before you need one, to locate a quality mechanic, plumber, or roofer, then should the need arise, you will have a list of businesses that you can contact.

Police Fraud

There is a certain type of fraud that seldom gets addressed in books dealing with hoaxes, scams, and frauds — police fraud. As children, we are taught that "the policeman is our friend" and that if we are in trouble we can call the police for help. In most cases, the police are honest and there to help.

They perform a job that can be tedious, thankless, and often dangerous. I certainly don't want to detract from what the honest men and women serving in our nation's law enforcement agencies do, but there is an undercurrent of dishonesty in many of these agencies that must not be overlooked.

Police routinely lie to cover up their violations of the constitutional rights and freedoms of suspects. In their pursuit of criminals, the police may take actions which violate the protections guaranteed us by the Constitution. Rather than see the "guilty" go free on a "technicality," police sometimes alter their reports and perjure themselves when providing testimony at trial. In an article concerning police perjury and fraud, "Testilying: Police Perjury and What To Do About It," in the *University of Colorado Law Review* (67 U. Colo. L. Rev. 1037), author Christopher Slobogin states: "There is strong evidence to suggest that police in many jurisdictions routinely engage in this kind of deceit, and that prosecutors and judges are sometimes accomplices to it." The article also refers to a study by Myron W. Orfield, Jr., "Deterrence, Perjury, and the Heater Factor: An Exclusionary Rule in the Chicago Criminal Courts," published earlier in the *University of Colorado Law Review* (63 U. Colo. L. Rev. 75, 107), stating:

> "Orfield's findings are based on the views of prosecutors and judges as well as those of defense attorneys. In his survey of these three groups (which together comprised twenty-seven to forty-one individuals, depending on the question), 52% believed that at least 'half of the time' the prosecutor 'knows or has reason to know' that police fabricate evidence at suppression hearings, and 93%, including 89% of the prosecutors,

stated that prosecutors had such knowledge of perjury 'at least some of the time.' Sixty-one percent, including 50% of the state's attorneys, believed that prosecutors know or have reason to know that police fabricate evidence in case reports, and 50% of the prosecutors believed the same with respect to warrants (despite the fact that many prosecutors refused to talk about this latter area)."

We see the same type of evidence reported by Marvin Zalman and Larry J. Siegel in their book *Criminal Procedure, Constitution and Society* (Belmont, CA: West/Wadsworth, 1995), in which they state: "police perjury is committed routinely and deliberately by police, typically in narcotics enforcement, to cover up the knowing and blatant disregard of the constitutional rules of conduct set out under the 4th Amendment and the rule against self-incrimination."

What does this mean to you? Assuming that these studies and reports are reasonably accurate, it means that if you have some type of adverse interaction with the police, it is likely that they will lie to aid in your conviction. Police officers are human; they can lie, exaggerate, and omit important facts as well as the next person. The problem is that when police lie, it can cost you much more than you realize.

Of course, the best way to avoid having to deal with the problem of police fraud is to avoid contact with the police. This is not always possible, because contact with the police can result from police error — they misidentify you, minor infractions — an inoperative taillight on your car, or something as simple as casual contact — you and the police just happen to be in the same place at the same time.

In any case where you have contact with the police beyond perhaps saying hello as you pass on the street, you must assume that the police suspect you of some crime or infraction. The police do not initiate contact with someone unless they believe that person is involved in some type of wrongdoing. However, like anyone else, the police can make mistakes.

When dealing with the police, it is essential that you retain all of your rights. If you are detained, you must never under any circumstances consent to any type of search of your vehicle or possessions. If you are arrested, you must never, under any circumstances, speak with the police about anything without the presence of your attorney. If you are given a written citation for some type of infraction, you should contest the citation in court. Doing these things does not mean that you are guilty or that you have something to hide. Rather, it means that you are using the rights and freedoms guaranteed to every American by the Constitution.

The American Civil Liberties Union (ACLU — www.aclu.org) has published a "Bust Card" detailing how one may safeguard one's rights when dealing with the police. Although you may not be strongly in favor of everything the ACLU has to say, the information in their Bust Card makes good sense. You can obtain a copy of the ACLU Bust Card on the Internet at:

www.aclu.org/issues/criminal/bustcardtext.html.

Conclusion

Throughout this book we have looked at several different types of hoaxes, scams, and frauds. We have discussed how some of these crimes work, and looked at things you can do to protect yourself from becoming a victim of these crimes.

As was stated in the beginning of the book, there is no way to discuss every possible hoax, scam, and fraud, but it is certainly possible to develop an awareness that will cause criminals to move on to an easier, less aware target. A few simple points to remember are:

- If a deal sounds too good to be true, it isn't true.

- If you have to pay in advance to receive a prize, it's a scam.

- If a stranger approaches you on the street needing help with a large sum of cash, you're being conned.

- If you receive an offer through unsolicited commercial e-mail (spam), it's a scam.

- If a stranger asks you to disclose personal and private information about yourself or your family, you may be a target for some type of crime.

- If someone calls your home wanting to sell you some item and asks you to provide your credit card number and billing information, it may be a scam or the beginning of credit card fraud. Even if you are dealing with a legitimate telemarketer, you may be providing personal information to a convicted felon.

To protect yourself from hoaxes, scams, frauds, identity theft, and related crimes, it is important to develop an attitude and mindset that works to safeguard your personal privacy. It is very difficult to successfully perpetrate these crimes against someone whom the criminal knows little about, and who consistently acts to safeguard his personal privacy. As with other criminals, the con man, the scam artist, and the identity thief will move on to easier and less aware targets if you take even the most basic steps to protect yourself. After all, there are many people who take no precautions at all — they make great victims.

Appendix
State Consumer Protection Agencies

Below are listed the state Consumer Protection Offices for all fifty states and the District of Columbia. In addition, many states also have district, regional, county, or city consumer protection offices. A complete list of these offices can be found on the Internet at:

www.pueblo.gsa.gov/crh/state.htm.

The Consumer Protection Offices of each state can provide you with information regarding the various hoaxes, scams, and frauds that are affecting that state or an area of the state. Furthermore, if you find that you have become a victim of some kind of hoax, scam, or fraud, these offices will be able to assist you in resolving the matter and perhaps recovering some of your losses.

However, it is always better to avoid becoming a victim of crime than to have to recover from being a victim. With this in mind, take time today to contact your state's Consumer Protection Office. Find out what resources they have available. What advice can they provide to help protect you and your family from hoaxes, scams, and fraud? What are the current hoaxes, scams, and frauds that criminals are perpetrating in your state, and what should you be aware of today?

Alabama
Consumer Affairs Division
Office of the Attorney General
11 South Union Street
Montgomery, AL 36130
334-242-7335
Toll free in AL: 1-800-392-5658
Web site: www.ago.state.al.us

Alaska
Consumer Protection Unit
Office of the Attorney General
1031 West 4th Avenue, Suite 200
Anchorage, AK 99501-5903
907-269-5100
Fax: 907-276-8554
Web site: www.law.state.ak.us

Arizona
Consumer Protection and Advocacy Section
Office of the Attorney General
1275 West Washington Street
Phoenix, AZ 85007
602-542-3702
602-542-5763 (consumer information and complaints)
Toll free in AZ: 1-800-352-8431
TDD: 602-542-5002
Fax: 602-542-4579
Web site: www.ag.state.az.us

Arkansas
Consumer Protection Division
Office of the Attorney General
323 Center Street, Suite 200
Little Rock, AR 72201
501-682-2341
Voice/TDD toll free in AR: 1-800-482-8982
Toll free: 1-800-482-8982
TDD: 501-682-6073
Fax: 501-682-8118
Web site: www.ag.state.ar.us
E-mail: consumer@ag.state.ar.us

California
California Department of Consumer Affairs
400 R Street, Suite 3000
Sacramento, CA 95814
916-445-4465
Toll free in CA: 1-800-952-5210
TDD/TTY: 916-322-1700
Web site: www.dca.ca.gov

Colorado
Consumer Protection Division
Colorado Attorney General's Office
1525 Sherman Street, 5th Floor
Denver, CO 80203-1760
303-866-5189
303-866-5125
Toll free: 1-800-222-4444
Fax: 303-866-5443
Web site: www.ago.state.co.us
E-mail: stop.fraud@state.co.us

Connecticut
Department of Consumer Protection
165 Capitol Avenue
Hartford, CT 06106
860-713-6300
Toll free in CT: 1-800-842-2649
Fax: 860-713-7239
Web site: www.state.ct.us/dcp/

Delaware
Consumer Protection Unit
Department of Justice
Carvel State Office Building
820 North French Street, 5th Floor
Wilmington, DE 19801
302-577-8600
Toll free in DE: 1-800-220-5424
Fax: 302-577-3090
Web site: www.state.de.us/attgen/consumer.htm
E-mail: orybakoff@state.de.us

District of Columbia
Office of the Corporation Counsel
441 4th Street NW, Suite 450 North
Washington, DC 20001
202-442-9828 (consumer hotline)
Fax: 202-727-6546
Web site: www.occ.dc.gov
E-Mail: consumercomplaint@dc.gov

Florida
Division of Consumer Services
2005 Apalachee Parkway
Rhodes Building
Tallahassee, FL 32399-6500
850-922-2966
Toll free in FL:1-800-435-7352
Fax: 850-410-3801
Web site: www.800helpfla.com

Georgia
Governor's Office of Consumer Affairs
2 Martin Luther King, Jr. Drive, Suite 356
Atlanta, GA 30334
404-651-8600
Toll free in GA (outside Atlanta area): 1-800-869-1123
Fax: 404-651-9018
Web site: www2.state.ga.us/gaoca

Hawaii
Office of Consumer Protection
Department of Commerce and Consumer Affairs
345 Kekuananoa Street, Suite 12
Hilo, HI 96720
808-933-0910
Fax: 808-933-8845
Web site: state.hi.us/dcca

Idaho
Consumer Protection Unit
Idaho Attorney General's Office
650 West State Street
Boise, ID 83720-0010
208-334-2424
Toll free in ID: 1-800-432-3545
Fax: 208-334-2830
Web site: www.state.id.us/ag

Illinois
Office of the Attorney General
500 South Second Street
Springfield, IL 62706
See Web site for toll free hotline numbers
Fax: 618-529-6416
Web site: www.ag.state.il.us

Indiana
Consumer Protection Division
Office of the Attorney General
402 West Washington Street, 5th Floor
Indianapolis, IN 46204
317-232-6330
Toll free in IN: 1-800-382-5516
Fax: 317-233-4393
Web site: www.in.gov/attorneygeneral/consumer

Iowa
Consumer Protection Division
Office of the Attorney General
1305 East Walnut Street
Des Moines, IA 50319
515-281-5926
Fax: 515-281-6771
Web site: www.state.ia.us/government/ag/consumer.html
E-mail: consumer@ag.state.ia.us

Kansas
Consumer Protection Division
Office of the Attorney General
120 SW 10th, 2nd Floor
Topeka, KS 66612-1597
785-296-3751
Toll free in KS: 1-800-432-2310
Fax: 785-291-3699
Web site: www.ink.org/public/ksag
E-mail: cprotect@ksag.org

Kentucky
Consumer Protection Division
Office of the Attorney General
9001 Shelbyville Road, Suite 3
Louisville, KY 40222
502-696-5389
Toll free in KY: 1-888-432-9257
Fax: 502-573-8317
Web site: www.law.state.ky.us/cp
E-mail: attorney.general@law.state.ky.us

Louisiana
Consumer Protection Section
Office of the Attorney General
301 Main Street, Suite 1250
Baton Rouge, LA 70801
225-342-9639
Toll free nationwide: 1-800-351-4889
Fax: 225-342-9637
Web site: www.ag.state.la.us

Maine
Maine Attorney General's Consumer Mediation Service
6 State House Station
Augusta, ME 04333
207-626-8800
Web site: www.state.me.us/ag

Maryland
Consumer Protection Division
Office of the Attorney General
200 Saint Paul Place, 16th Floor
Baltimore, MD 21202-2021
410-528-8662 (consumer complaint hotline)
410-576-6550 (consumer information)
TDD: 410-576-6372 (Maryland only)
Fax: 410-576-7040
Web site: www.oag.state.md.us/consumer
E-mail: consumer@oag.state.md.us

Massachusetts

Executive Office of Consumer Affairs and Business Regulation
One Ashburton Place, Room 1411
Boston, MA 02108
617-727-7780 (information and referral only)
TDD/TTY: 617-727-1729
Fax: 617-227-6094
Web site: www.state.ma.us/consumer
E-mail: consumer@state.ma.us

Michigan

Consumer Protection Division
Office of Attorney General
PO Box 30213
Lansing, MI 48909
517-373-1140 (complaint information)
517-373-1110
Fax: 517-335-1935
Web site: www.ag.state.mi.us/cp

Minnesota

Consumer Services Division
Minnesota Attorney General's Office
1400 NCL Tower
445 Minnesota Street
St. Paul, MN 55101
612-296-3353
Toll free: 1-800-657-3787
Fax: 612-282-5801
Web site: www.ag.state.mn.us/consumer
E-mail: consumer.ag@state.mn.us

Mississippi
Consumer Protection
Division of the Mississippi Attorney General's Office
PO Box 22947
Jackson, MS 39225-2947
601-359-4230
Toll free in MS: 1-800-281-4418
Fax: 601-359-4231
Web site: www.ago.state.ms.us/consprot.htm

Missouri
Consumer Protection and Trade Offense Division
PO Box 899
1530 Rax Court
Jefferson City, MO 65102
573-751-6887
573-751-3321
Toll free in MO: 1-800-392-8222
TDD/TTY toll free in MO: 1-800-729-8668
Fax: 573-751-7948
Web site: www.ago.state.mo.us
E-mail: attgenmail@moago.org

Montana
Consumer Affairs Unit
Department of Commerce
1424 Ninth Avenue
Box 200501
Helena, MT 59620-0501
406-444-4312
Fax: 406-444-2903
Web site: www.state.mt.us/doa/consumerprotection

Nebraska
Department of Justice
2115 State Capitol
PO Box 98920
Lincoln, NE 68509
402-471-2682
Toll free: 1-800-727-6432
Fax: 402-471-3297
Web site: www.nol.org/home/ago

Nevada
Nevada Consumer Affairs Division
1850 East Sahara, Suite 101
Las Vegas, NV 89104
702-486-7355
Web site: www.fyiconsumer.org

New Hampshire
Consumer Protection and Antitrust Bureau
New Hampshire Attorney General's Office
33 Capitol Street
Concord, NH 03301
603-271-3641
TDD toll free: 1-800-735-2964
Fax: 603-271-2110
Web site: www.state.nh.us/nhdoj/Consumer/cpb.html

New Jersey
Department of Law and Public Safety
New Jersey Division of Consumer Affairs
PO Box 45025
Newark, NJ 07101
973-504-6200
Toll free in NJ: 1-800-242-5846
Web site: www.state.nj.us/lps/ca/home.htm
E-mail: askconsumeraffairs@smtp.lps.state.nj.us

New Mexico
Consumer Protection Division
Office of the Attorney General
PO Drawer 1508
407 Galisteo
Santa Fe, NM 87504-1508
505-827-6060
Toll free in NM: 1-800-678-1508
Fax: 505-827-6685
Web site: www.ago.state.nm.us

New York
Bureau of Consumer Frauds and Protection
Office of the Attorney General
State Capitol
Albany, NY 12224
518-474-5481
Toll free in NY: 1-800-771-7755 (hotline)
Fax: 518-474-3618
Web site: www.oag.state.ny.us

North Carolina
Consumer Protection Section
Office of the Attorney General
PO Box 629
Raleigh, NC 27602
919-716-6000
Fax: 919-716-6050
Web site: www.jus.state.nc.us/cpframe.htm

North Dakota
Consumer Protection and Antitrust Division
Office of the Attorney General
600 East Boulevard Avenue, Department 125
Bismarck, ND 58505-0040
701-328-3404
Toll free in ND: 1-800-472-2600
TTY: 800-366-6888
Fax: 701-328-3535
Web site: www.ag.state.nd.us/ndag/cpat/cpat.html
E-mail: cpat@state.nd.us

Ohio
Ohio Attorney General's Office
30 East Broad Street, 25th Floor
Columbus, OH 43215-3428
614-466-8831
Toll free in OH: 1-800-282-0515
TDD: 614-466-1393
Fax: 614-728-7583
Web site: www.ag.state.oh.us
E-mail: consumer@ag.state.oh.us

Oklahoma
Consumer Protection Unit
4545 North Lincoln Blvd., Suite 260
Oklahoma City, OK 73105
405-521-2029
Toll free: 1-800-448-4904
Fax: 405-528-1867
Web site: www.oag.state.ok.us

Oregon
Financial Fraud/Consumer Protection Section
Department of Justice
1162 Court Street NE
Salem, OR 97310
503-378-4732
503-378-4320 (hotline Salem only)
503-229-5576 (hotline Portland only)
Toll free in OR: 1-877-877-9392
TDD/TTY: 503-378-5939
Fax: 503-378-5017
Web site: www.doj.state.or.us

Pennsylvania
Consumer Advocate
Office of the Consumer Advocate
Office of the Attorney General
Forum Place, 5th Floor
Harrisburg, PA 17101-1921
717-783-5048 (utilities only)
Toll free in PA: 1-800-684-6560
Fax: 717-783-7152
Web site: www.oca.state.pa.us
E-mail: paoca@ptd.net

Rhode Island
Consumer Unit
Consumer Protection Unit
Department of Attorney General
150 South Main Street
Providence, RI 02903
401-274-4400
Toll free in RI: 1-800-852-7776
TDD: 401-453-0410
Fax: 401-222-5110
Web site: www.riag.state.ri.us/consumer

South Carolina
State Ombudsman
Office of Executive Policy and Program
1205 Pendleton Street, Room 308
Columbia, SC 29201
803-734-0457
Toll free in SC only: 1-800-686-0040
Fax: 803-734-0546
Web site: www.state.sc.us

South Dakota
Director of Consumer Affairs
Office of the Attorney General
500 East Capitol
State Capitol Building
Pierre, SD 57501-5070
605-773-4400
Toll free in SD: 1-800-300-1986
TDD: 605-773-6585
Fax: 605-773-7163

Tennessee
Division of Consumer Affairs
500 James Robertson Parkway, 5th Floor
Nashville, TN 37243-0600
615-741-4737
Toll free in TN: 1-800-342-8385
Fax: 615-532-4994
Web site: www.state.tn.us/consumer

Texas
Consumer Protection Division
Office of Attorney General
PO Box 12548
Austin, TX 78711-2548
512-463-2070
Fax: 512-463-8301
Web site: www.oag.state.tx.us

Utah

Division of Consumer Protection
Department of Commerce
160 East 300 South
Box 146704
Salt Lake City, UT 84114-6704
801-530-6601
Fax: 801-530-6001
Web site: www.commerce.state.ut.us
E-mail: commerce@br.state.ut.us

Vermont

Consumer Assistance Program
For Consumer Complaints & Questions
104 Morrill Hall
UVM
Burlington, VT 05405
802-656-3183 (within Chittenden County or out of state)
Toll free in VT: 1-800-649-2424
Web site: www.state.vt.us/atg

Virginia

Office of Consumer Affairs
Department of Agriculture and Consumer Services
Washington Building, Suite 100
PO Box 1163
Richmond, VA 23219
804-786-2042
Toll free in VA: 1-800-552-9963
TDD: 800-828-1120
Fax: 804-371-7479
Web site: www.vdacs.state.va.us

Washington
Consumer Resource Center
Office of the Attorney General
905 Plum Street, Bldg. 3
PO Box 40118
Olympia, WA 98504-0118
360-753-6210
Web site: www.wa.gov/ago

West Virginia
Consumer Protection Division
Office of the Attorney General
812 Quarrier Street, 6th Floor
PO Box 1789
Charleston, WV 25326-1789
304-558-8986
Toll free in WV: 1-800-368-8808
Fax: 304-558-0184
Web site: www.state.wv.us/wvag
E-mail: consumer@wvnet.edu

Wisconsin
Division of Trade and Consumer Protection
Department of Agriculture
Trade and Consumer Protection
3610 Oakwood Hills Parkway
Eau Claire, WI 54701-7754
715-839-3848
Toll free in WI: 1-800-422-7128
Fax: 715-839-1645
Web site: www.datcp.state.wi.us

```
Appendix
State Consumer Protection Agencies


143
```

Wyoming
Office of the Attorney General
Consumer Protection Unit
123 State Capitol Building
Cheyenne, WY 82002
307-777-7874
Toll free in WY only: 1-800-438-5799
Fax: 307-777-7956
Web site: www.state.wy.us/~ag/consumer.htm

YOU WILL ALSO WANT TO READ:

☐ **58148 MODERN FRAUDS AND CON GAMES, by Tony Lesce.** Fraud is the fastest growing industry in the world, which is why it has become a global trillion-dollar problem. The main reason is that it's low-risk compared to other crimes. This volume describes dozens of frauds, many of which are not illegal, but do involve deception for economic gain. This book will shed new light on the new frauds and con games, with an extensive chapter on steps you can take to reduce your vulnerability to fraud. No book on fraud can be the final word, but this will help you protect yourself and your family. *2002, 5½ x 8½, 200 pp, soft cover. $15.00.*

☐ **40091 21ST CENTURY FRAUD, How to Protect Yourself in the New Millennium, by Tony Lesce.** This book will show you the basics of fraud techniques, give you an awareness of what the dangers are, and teaches you how to protect yourself against the possibility that a fraud artist might fleece you. Included: organized crime; telephone scams; credit card fraud; computer and internet fraud; retail store scams; fund-raising organizations; and much, much more. *2000, 5½ x 8½, 160 pp, soft cover. $15.95.*

☐ **61163 IDENTITY THEFT, The Cybercrime of the Millennium, by John Q. Newman.** Your most valuable possession is not your house, your car, or your collection of antique jewelry. Your most valuable possession is what makes you *you* — your identity. What would happen if someone stole it? Each year, more than 500,000 Americans fall victim to identity theft, and that number is rising. A stolen identity can mean the loss of your job, your credit rating, your friends, and in extreme cases, can result in a prison sentence for a crime you did not commit. This book is the most effective tool in your arsenal against the cybercrime grifter. Use it to protect your identity — while you still have one. *1999, 5½ x 8½, 100 pp, soft cover. $12.00.*

☐ **61168 THE ID FORGER: Homemade Birth Certificates & Other Documents Explained, by John Q. Newman.** *The ID Forger* covers in step-by-step detail all of the classic and modern high-tech methods of forging the commonly used identification documents; old-fashioned forgery; computer forgery; birth certificate basics; and other miscellaneous document forgery. *Sold for information purposes only. 1999, 5½ x 8½, 110 pp, soft cover. $15.00.*

☐ **61174 FAKE ID BY MAIL AND MODEM, by Trent Sands.** Thanks to the wonders of computer technology, fake ID is better than ever before! ID cards such as driver's licenses, Social Security cards, union cards, employee and student cards are so real-looking that only seasoned professional ID checkers can tell the difference! And thanks to the Internet, suppliers of fake ID are all over the place. Topics covered include: what kinds of ID are available and who sells them; what fake ID should and should not be used for; how to "customize" your mail-order ID; and much, much more. *Sold for informational purposes only. 2000, 5½ x 8, 102 pp, soft cover. $12.00.*

☐ **61164 HOW TO MAKE DRIVER'S LICENSES AND OTHER ID ON YOUR HOME COMPUTER, by Max Forgé.** Sometimes you just need to fake it. Author Max Forgé brings liberation to the technology front with this step-by-step manual that tells you everything you need to know about making your own ID cards at home. This book covers how to download software and license templates off the Internet; the best equipment to use; how to add holograms and other "anti-counterfeiting" devices; printing, cutting, laminating, and much more. Bring the power of technology home with this book and do it yourself — the right way. *Sold for informational purposes only. 1999, 5½ x 8½, 96 pp, illustrated, soft cover. $12.00.*

☐ **40093 THE REAL WORK, Essential Sleight of Hand for Street Operators, by Paul Price.** After becoming bored with creating illusions for children's birthday parties, Paul Price witnessed a game of Three Card Monte on the wharves of San Francisco. The following weekend, armed with his magician's knowledge of sleight of hand, our author threw away his magician's cloak and went to work on the streets. His first day netted him $200. After reading **The Real Work**, you will no longer be among the mindless mass of followers. You will have the power to profit from the public's simplemindedness. Use it wisely. *Sold for informational and educational purposes only. 2001, 5½ x 8½, 80 pp, illustrated, soft cover. $12.00.*

☐ **58080 THE PRIVACY POACHERS, How the Government and Big Corporations Gather, Use, and Sell Information About You, *by Tony Lesce.*** This book explains how various snoops get their hands on sensitive information about you, such as your financial records, medical history, legal records and much more. Government and private snoops can combine data from financial transactions by using taps, mail monitoring, and other surveillance methods. This information is then packaged and sold, over and over again, without your consent. Find out what the Privacy Poachers have on you, and what you can do to protect yourself. *1992, 5½ x 8½, 155 pp, soft cover. $16.95.*

We offer the very finest in controversial and unusual books — check out the catalog ad on the next page.

Loompanics Unlimited
PO Box 1197
Port Townsend, WA 98368

DBV2

Please send me the books I have checked above. I have enclosed $_____ which includes $5.95 for shipping and handling of the first $25.00 ordered. Add an additional $1 shipping for each additional $25 ordered. Washington residents include 8.2% sales tax.

Name _____

Address _____

City/State/Zip_____

We accept VISA, Discover, and MasterCard. To place a credit card order *only,* call 1-800-380-2230, 24 hours a day, 7 days a week. Or fax your credit card order to 360-385-7785. Or order online at www.loompanics.com